W9-ACN-287

GROWING UP IN INDIA

THE MINERVA ASSOCIATES
7-B, Lake Place : Calcutta-29

First Published : February 1972

Price : Rs. 20.00

Printed in India by R. M. Banerjee Printer, 22 R. G. Kar Road, Calcutta 4 and Published by T. K. Mukherjee, on behalf of The Minerva Associates, 7-B, Lake Place, Calcutta-29.

Growing Up in India

PRADIP BOSE

THE MINERVA ASSOCIATES

To

Joyce,

With love

"Life is action and passion; therefore it is required of a man that he should share the passion and action of his time at peril of being judged not to have lived."

—Justice Oliver Wendell Holmes

"When I came to the world, everybody laughed and I cried. When I die, let me laugh and everybody cry."

—Tulsidas

CONTENTS

PART ONE

NATIONAL MEMORIES

CHAPTER I

"The great revelations a man receives in his life are few, usually one or two. But they transfigure him, like his luck".
—Albert Camus.

I was thirteen years old at that time and it was the first summer we had lived among the dust and rocks of Santhal Parganas. Our house was isolated, standing in the midst of a forest. In the hot nights we slept out under the huge blazing stars, waking with the dawn chorus of birds to a delightful pristine coolness. But as the sun climbed above the horizon, sucking up the dews, every creature ran to take shelter from the devouring heat. Doors and windows were shut tightly against the glare, and water thrown on cement floors to keep them cool.

We three children, Partho, Lalita and myself, spent the whole day at home, for it was the summer holidays. During the long airless afternoons my parents and the three of us gathered in the dark sitting room to sleep away the hours of unbearable heat; the sulky silence was broken only by the hand *punkha* pulled by the servant sitting out on the verandah. Frieda, our Alsatian, stayed with us, gasping in the heat and stretching full length on the floor trying to absorb as much coolness as possible.

How I detested those stifling hours! Yet there was no escape. Severe reprimand greeted any attempt to creep away and after three hours we were all eager for any activity which meant freedom once more.

One day, after the rest period ended, we had taken cool drinks and fruit and then with Frieda bounding along in front, set out in the company of Haradhan, our servant. I remember the rains had not yet arrived and the earth was split and cracked by the sun. We took a path along the tracks of the bullock carts through the *sal* forest and passed a well-kept vegetable garden which had recently been watered, the smell of the wet ground filling the air with coolness. Then leaving the forest we found the sloping ground falling away to a small brook, and in the distance, on the other side, a village with mud huts and thatched roofs.

Eagerly we threw away our shoes and ran to play in the sparkling water until Haradhan suddenly said: "That is my village over there, would you like to come and see my house?"

Now, although I had, of course, seen villages from trains and cars, I had never really visited one. I had none of the intimate knowledge which comes from actually passing through a place on foot, being close to the houses, in contact with passers-by. I suppose the nearest experience was the family's annual visit to our village home at Kodalia, situated about eleven miles away from the centre of Calcutta. But even this was not a typical village for there were a number of brick buildings which gave it more urban character. Moreover, our visits there were always during the Puja festivities in the autumn, when the prevailing mood was different, gayer, less weighed down by the mundane, day-to-day problems of existence.

We would arrive in a cavalcade of four or five cars and as soon as the first entered the village, groups of small children would come running and follow us, calling and shouting. As we left the cars, dressed in our best clothes for the festive occasion, we basked in the attention of the young and old alike, who regarded us with a mixture of awe, curiosity and admiration. But generally we stayed aloof, swimming in the family tank and picnicking in the garden, returning to Calcutta before the evening to join the festivities there. But on such occasions we thought only of our own pleasure. The village people lived in another world and we had no interest in their problems and how they passed their lives.

The village to which Haradhan was now pointing looked like any one of thousand villages that I had seen from the distance. I was eager to catch a glimpse of the place where some of our servants lived although I had heard of the indescribable poverty which existed there. Full of curiosity we followed him. Haradhan's house, with mud walls and thatched roof, was the first one that we came to. He led us through the little courtyard, passed a cowshed, by a dug-in oven on which a meal was being cooked and onto a small verandah which led into a dark and airless room. A pall of smoke hung over everything. In the dim interior I could distinguish a few kitchen utensils, brass and enamel plates, two or three cots woven from coconut ropes and miscellaneous pieces of ragged clothing hanging here and there. There seemed no escaping from the smell of the cow-shed. I suddenly felt stifled in that hot oppressive atmosphere.

Haradhan's mother appeared out of the smoky gloom, obviously ill-at-ease with her unexpected guests. She offered food but we hastily refused and retreated with relief into the open air. But the relief was shortlived. Our appearance in the street along with the dog, immediately attracted the attention of an excited crowd of children, who came running forward, jostling and pushing, their high pitched chatter mingling with the chorus of howling village dogs, but I was dimly aware of them. It was the sight of the filth, the dust, the flies, the pitiful degradation and squalor which held my horrified gaze and engraved itself on my mind.

Looking back, I should say that we perhaps spent about twenty minutes in that village before returning to our house, yet those twenty minutes changed my life. It was as though I was born again, this time with my eyes wide open to the poverty and suffering which disfigured the face of India like an open sore.

The days which followed still remain vividly in my memory. That evening we slept again under the stars, lulled by the monotonous drum-beating of the Santhals. Try as I would, I could not banish the experience of the afternoon from my thoughts. Again and again the picture of the thin, dirty, neglected children forced itself upon me. I tried to drive it away by thinking of happier things but it was of no use. Night after night I was haunted by this same vision until at last the full realization of what this experience would mean was forced upon me. All the dreams and delights which had occupied so large a space in my boyish thought—to become a man of learning, to possess a modern house with a large swimming pool and a fine library and to own a red sports car, would, I could see, have now to be relinquished. They could not exist side by side with the new image which obsessed me.

Having seen with my own eyes the tragedy of India I could no longer remain inactive in the face of it. The situation was not such that it could be easily dismissed by the tossing of a few coins to solve the troubled conscience. The clutching fingers of the village children were too insistent to be dislodged in so simple a fashion. Yet instinctively I shrank from a commitment which would involve so much uprooting of the old ways and ideas. I began to dread going to bed. During the daytime my mind could be diverted in a hundred ways but night left my brain whirling with a thousand questions. At last one night I could bear the pain of non-commitment no longer. It was as though I had reached the end of a long and wearisome journey. I had made up my mind and to myself I made a vow : "I will try to do something to change the lives of these afflicted people". An immense feeling of relief flooded over me and for the first time for days I fell peacefully asleep.

Years afterwards the reason for both the pain and tranquility which I experienced seemed clearer to me than they did at the time. The pain was not caused entirely by what I had seen in the village but was also related to the disintegration of all the values which, until then, I had held to be worthwhile. Tranquility was achieved when, looking back, I seemed to perceive in the face of the village children a reflection of my own. Their sufferings were mine. Although my suffering was of a different kind yet we seemed to belong to the same community of suffering and neglected people. Some deep centre of my being was touched and awakened and though the process of transition from the desire to escape, to the final, total response was indescribably painful, it was in this response I eventually discovered all that a man seeks in life as justification for his existence : emotional warmth, intellectual satisfaction and spiritual renewal.

The reason why I was apparently so much affected by this experience, when my brother and sister, both brought up in the same environment, subjected to the same influences, remained unmoved, can I think be explained by an incident which had happened in my early childhood.

One day my brother, Partho and I were playing in one of the upper rooms of our Elgin Road house when my grandmother's cook, appeared.

"Parthodadababu, your grandmother is asking for you. Will you please come now ?", he said. Partho stood up and without waiting to enquire the reason followed Sarbeswar down the stairs which led to my grandmother's room. Full of curiosity I followed. When we entered she was sitting there on the *ashan* with the simple widow's meal before her.

"You have come," she said greeting my brother, "Sit there and eat", and indicated the place on her right where more food had been placed.

I stood at a loss in the doorway filled with embarrasment. I had come there in all innocence but found myself in a place where I was clearly not wanted. My grandmother had looked up but her glance went straight through me as though I did not exist. Partho looked at me pleadingly. Obviously he would have liked to share the meal with me but before so august a person he would never have dared make such a suggestion. I felt rooted to the spot in misery and helplessness. After some moments of acute indecision I tore myself away and ran back to my room where I fell upon the bed and sobbed.

This was the climax of a whole series of similar occurrences which made me know for certain that I was in some way different, less likeable, of less value than the others in my family; and I knew why. It was all on account of the colour of my skin.

It is not necessary to delve very deeply into the ethnological and cultural history of India to arrive at some understanding of my grandmother's prejudices. One might say that from the time of the Aryan conquest to the period of British raj, it has been the lighter skinned conquerors who have dominated the scene of northern part of the sub-continent. Conquest brings with it associative ideas of superiority and the consequent desire of the vanquished to ape the conquerors and to partake of their "superior" nature (just as the conquered Britons tried to colour their skin to look like the Romans). It is not surprising therefore that during three thousand years of history the concept of white skin superiority penetrated the consciousness of the people of northern India.

To be fair-skinned was to be more beautiful or by implication a better or a more superior being. To be a father of a number of dark-skinned daughters was one of the greatest misfortunes that could befall a man because only a handsome dowry would persuade a prospective bridegroom to accept so great a liability. The upper classes in their anxiety to keep the lineage as fair as possible would often marry their sons to the fair daughters of much poorer families.

Against such a background my grandmother made her

choice. Her liking for her grandchildren increased according to the fairness of their complexion. In the environment in which I grew up I was comparatively dark-skinned and consequently so low down in her list that I hardly existed at all in her estimation. But the fact that she was the eldest in the family and much respected by everyone, was sufficient to convince me that I was a person of very little worth. In addition, I do not think I could have been a particularly bright or an expressive child. Consequently, although I felt at ease with my contemporaries (left to themselves, children are seldom colour-conscious) I quickly developed an acute sense of inferiority, particularly in relation to my elders. These remote, all-powerful beings were, I thought, beyond being influenced in their attitude towards me. Their minds were already made up. Yet I yearned desperately for any small attention and praise which would give me confidence in myself.

After my grandmother's rejection it seemed that I was imprisoned in the shackles of inferiority and alienation. From that time I set myself the task of subjecting all my relationships with others to a close and persistent scrutiny. With my brother, Partho, I felt safe. He showed warm protective feelings towards me, and we were great friends. My sister, Lalita, was fond of me. Romanath, the servant who looked after us and to whom we were greatly attached called me "bhalodadababu" — the good boy. So at least in my immediate family circle there seemed to be no evidence of discrimination.

But the most crucial relationship was with my mother. She belonged to the ranks of the "fearful elders", whose attitudes could not be altered by even the most prodigious efforts on my part. I was painfully anxious to discover any element of favouritism or rejection on her part. And yet somehow I think she understood my problem. For although she was extremely fair to all her children, she did, I think, give me that extra affection that was necessary to establish faith in myself. And so it was, that while I existed in alien world in which it seemed many antagonistic forces were piled against me, there was in the very centre of my existence a solid warmth, which gave me the confidence to face this youthful emotional crisis.

It was then with all these feelings of basic insecurity and disillusion about the world around me, alleviated to some extent by my mother's love, that I grew from childhood to adolescence. After the walk through Haradhan's village however, I found that I was able to free myself from the purely personal preoccupation with my own difficulties. I acquired the capacity to objectify myself. I was convinced that in comparison with the sufferings of the children in that village my problems were infinitesimal. I learnt to have a sense of proportion and with this submergence of my individual troubles into the vast scheme of human suffering, came a compelling sense of purpose.

When I awoke the next morning it was not the same world in which I had fallen asleep. The world was different because I was different. What had so long seemed important and delightful to me were now dust and ashes. Thoughts and feelings of which I had previously been unaware now became vital. Looking back on my past life I rejected it completely. To work for one's own interest seemed to me a sin of which I must never be found guilty.

When the obsession with my own guilt and responsibility had receded a little, I found myself looking around me with more perception and curiosity than I had ever done before. What I saw filled me with confusion. My indifference had been the result, I knew, of ignorance. I simply had not known or imagined what life was like for the majority of Indian people. But ignorance could not be the reason for all the apathy and criminal indifference which I now realised existed everywhere. Even those I liked or respected among my relatives and friends seemed blind or were prepared to rationalise their indifference towards the grim realities of life in India.

The world appeared to be divided into the 'haves' and the 'have-nots' in the realm of sensitivity and the 'have-nots' it seemed were in the overwhelming majority. In fact, the whole society appeared to be organised in such a way that the entire social process tended to perpetuate the situation. There was no alternative but to reject wholly the existing order and its values and to become a full-fledged rebel. Now I felt a different kind of alienation from society from that I had previously known, but it was purposeful and even satisfying.

I was not, however, by temperament or capability a dashing revolutionary, for I was a rather shy, introverted and brooding type of boy. Yet my conviction that it was a cruel and dreadful world which must by some means be altered was unshakeable and I was prepared to give my life, if some part at least of this ambition could be realised. This sacrificial mood enveloped me. I burnt with sublime purpose and intellectual arrogance because it seemed that I alone had grasped "reality" in its all nakedness with every fibre of my being. Any criticism levelled against my ideas I would dismiss contemptuously. I was wiser than all my unsympathetic and unseeing elders : I would laugh at them silently, submerged as they were in the morass of indifference, conservatism and reaction.

However, my awakened consciousness responded wholeheartedly to both people and books in a way which cut across barriers of nation and language, customs and culture. Human suffering was the same everywhere. Those who laboured to reduce it were brothers whatever their race or creed.

Although those days which followed my walk in summer afternoon through the village were perhaps the most agonising I have ever experienced, yet I would not have them erased, for all the treasure in the world, for out of the pain, emerged a new purpose and a new will which were to be the foundation upon which my life was to be reconstructed.

CHAPTER II

"The desire and will of the leaders of India to win national independence represented the political ambition of many a generations of India's people."—A. Seifriz.

That same summer of 1941, when my careless childhood came to an end, was a period of comparative quiet on the Indian political scene, where, since 1938, I had as it were a front seat, to watch the drama being enacted. In that year, my uncle, Subhas Chandra Bose was elected the President of the Indian National Congress, the highest honour that nationalist India could bestow upon an Indian.

In spite of our pleadings we children were left behind when the rest of the family left for the Haripura Congress where the crowning ceremony was to take place during the annual conference of the Indian National Congress. But when they all returned we gathered round eagerly to hear their accounts of what had happened. The previous two years Jawaharlal Nehru had been the president of the Congress and consequently it was his turn to hand over the honour to my uncle. Since it was the 51st session of the Congress, great efforts had been made to symbolise it in different ways. We listened open mouthed to the description of the 51 gates of welcome and of the Presidential carriage, elaborately decorated, drawn by 51 bullocks. Enthusiastic crowds had gathered in their thousands and everyone in our family seemed delighted with the obvious popularity of the new president.

After my uncle's return to Calcutta, our family house in Elgin Road became, almost overnight, the centre of political activity. Distinguished people, foreign journalists, visitors of all kinds came and went in an ever flowing stream during the time that he remained there. During this period the highest body of the Congress, the Working Committee, comprising the top nationalist leaders from all parts of the country met, and Sardar Patel, Dr. Rajendra Prasad, Sm. Sarojini Naidu, Abul Kalam Azad, Khan Gaffar Khan, J. B. Kripalani became familiar figures. On several occasions Mahatma Gandhi and Jawaharlal

Nehru came and stayed at my uncle Sarat Bose's house at Woodburn Park. In those days we were drawn to the place as though by a magnet. One evening Rabindranath Tagore came to see Gandhi at the Woodburn Park house. On this occasion, with a few other children, we crept softly onto the verandah and peeping through the doors into one of the rooms, saw Tagore, with white flowing beard and cream coloured garments, sitting in an armchair, serene and composed, with Gandhi sitting cross-legged at his feet. As usual we had our autograph books ready. But we felt hesitant; we should be disturbing their conversation and would bring down a severe scolding upon our heads if we were found out. However, the temptation to obtain the signature of India's two most famous men was irresistible. After some urgent consultation we decided that our friend, Jagadish, should go in alone and then if he were caught, being a stranger he would be spared a more rigorous punishment. So gathering his courage he marched smartly in. Outside we craned our necks to see what would happen, holding our breath in silent expectation. We saw Tagore take the book in his hand and sign his name and then he handed it over to Gandhi. As a rule Gandhi would never give his autograph without taking Rs. 5/- for Harijan funds, but on this occasion he submitted to Tagore's plea and Jagadish emerged triumphantly with a free autograph from Gandhi!

It was not only political figures who were among the visitors. Others came representing many different spheres of Indian life. I can remember, among others, Sir C. V. Raman, Nobel Prize winner in Physics; Dr. S. Radhakrishnan, the philosopher; Sir P. C. Ray, the chemist. The immense power and versatility inherent in the Indian people seemed personified in this array of distinguished men and symbolised in the figure of the Congress President himself. Young as I was, it was impossible not to feel the great events were taking place and that we were lucky to be able to watch from such close quarters.

We, children, could not understand all the implication of what was happening, but as the weeks passed we could examine with great pride the galaxy of names which filled the pages of our autograph books. Three things however were clear to us: that we, the family, and most of our visitors and many unseen thousands who belonged to the world beyond our house composed a solid core of opposition to the British government, and would not rest until our country was free and independent. Then, from the immense crowds which always gathered around the leaders we understood that it was a movement not without considerable strength. It was taken for granted that association with this movement might involve danger, imprisonment and suffering.

As 1938 was nearing its end we heard much talk about the differences developing between my uncle and the right wing of the Congress, led by Mahatma Gandhi. During his visit to Europe in 1937-38 he was convinced that the clouds of war gathering over Europe would soon burst, and that in such circumstances India should press her claim for independence. It was an outright policy of "England's difficulty is India's opportunity". Knowing that it was the intention of the right wing to attempt some form of compromise with British imperialism, a policy to which he was firmly opposed, he was of the opinion that in order to forestall such a move a leftist President should be elected for 1939. He proposed the name of the Congress Socialist Party leader Acharya Narendra Deva, but it was the unanimous conclusion of the left wing that he himself should again stand for the Presidency.

This proposal was firmly opposed by the right wing who came out in open support of Dr. P. Sitaramayya. It was obvious that there was going to be a major power struggle between the left wing and the right wing within the Congress.

The day of the Congress Presidential election, the first in its history, was one of great suspense and excitement. On that day there was a garden party held on the occasion of my cousin, Asoke's marriage and my uncle attended this in spite of the pressure of events. Inside all was festivity and rejoicing. The tennis courts of Calcutta South Club situated next to uncle's house had been arranged with small tables to seat a thousand guests at the tea party. But inside the house the press correspondents had gathered like vultures. The telephone rang ceaselessly. The results of the voting soon came pouring in from all parts of the country. Growing bored with presenting the guests with tiny bouquets and garlands, I crept away into the house and was soon excitedly noting down meaningless digits in the same way that boys collect tram and car numbers. It was some hours before I was missed but when many results were yet to come, I was dragged away unwillingly to our Elgin Road house as it was quite late and the party had ended.

The next day the final result was known : my uncle got 1580 votes and his right wing rival 1375. We had won ! It was tremendous victory.

Soon afterwards Gandhi issued a statement saying : "I rejoice in this defeat" because he had openly supported Sitaramayya, but the part of the statement which read "After all, Subhas Bose is not an enemy of his country" aroused the greatest resentment among Bose's followers and in our family circle.

In later years, I understood that "rejoicing in defeat" was a mere Gandhian form of expression because there was certainly no joy in what he had said earlier : "I am nothing if I do not represent definite principles and policy. Therefore it is plain to me that the delegates do not approve of the principles and policy for which I stand." He admitted that "Subhas Chandra Bose instead of being the President on the sufferance of those whom he calls the rightists is now the President elected in a contested election". But it was Gandhi's threat to leave the Congress which held the most important political implication. He said: "In his (Bose's) opinion, his is the most forward and boldest policy and programme. The minority can only wish it all success. If they cannot keep pace with it, they must come out of it."

The election results had completely upset the status quo within the Congress. The unquestioned leader of the Congress for nearly two decades, Gandhi suddenly became the spokesman of the minority opinion within it! He had for so long been at the top of a ladder, of which Nehru occupied the second rung and Bose the third. Now Nehru had to retreat to third place and in a democratic election within Congress, Gandhi occupied the second position. The Indian political scene became pregnant with great uncertainty. Everything hinged on the question : how will Gandhi take his defeat ?

Bose expressed regret that Gandhi should have taken the result as a personal slight, and added that it would always be his aim to win Gandhi's confidence. But his plea for unity within Congress was in vain. For so long the right wing had dominated the Congress while tolerating the left wing minority, but now on the basis of a free and democratic election the position was reversed. At least for the next period the left wing had the majority and should have tolerated the right wing minority. That is what Bose wanted as the basis of unity, but the right wing, led by Gandhi, refused to play the game.

Looking back one may find valid reasons for criticising Gandhi and his followers on the ground that they refused to accept the normal procedure of democracy. But it would not be correct to do so because Gandhi never pretended that he was a democract in the modern sense of the term. He wanted to pursue his own truth and acknowledge a mystical "inner voice" as his guide rather than relying, on empirical facts and logical deduction. He was a messiah and not a conventional politician, hidebound with the cumbersome procedure of a modern democratic party. At least on this occasion he decided to take up the rule of a prophet. He was quite right when he surmised that Bose had within him the capacity to carry both the country and the Congress with him. If that was allowed then it would have meant complete defeat for Gandhian policy and principles and the victory for the policy of uncompromising anti-imperialist struggle combined with a revolutionary socialist outlook.

A later scrutiny of the events which occurred from 1938 onwards has led me to the conclusion that from the middle 'thirties Gandhi realised that it would be from Bose that the real challenge to his leadership would come one day and it was with this in mind that he attempted to repeat the tactics in 1938 which he had employed a decade earlier with much success, when a similar challenge had been launched by Jawaharlal Nehru. By deliberately arranging for Bose's election as the President of the Congress in 1938, he hoped thereby to obtain his allegiance and co-operation in his own future policies.

In 1927, after his return from abroad, which included a visit to the Soviet Union, Nehru became the acknowledged leader of the radical section of Congress, which at that time was increasing its popular appeal throughout the country, and potentially he was capable of challenging Gandhi's leadership both politically and ideologically. The main issue being debated then was on the question : Dominion Status or Complete Independence ? The Independence League, within the Congress, with Nehru as the President and Bose as the General Secretary was convinced that the aim of Dominion Status could never hold sufficient appeal to inspire young people to make sacrifices for its fulfillment. Only complete independence and the severance of all ties with British imperialism could do that. But Gandhi was entirely opposed to this view. At the Calcutta Congress in 1928 this issue was pressed by the radical section, and although it was finally voted down, the amendment collected enough support for Gandhi to realise that his leadership would be jeopardised at the next conference unless he was able to manipulate events in such way that while appearing to compromise with the popular demand he was also fortifying his own position.

Consequently for the 1929 Congress he adopted different tactics. He declared that unless the British government indicated its good intentions by the end of 1929, then he himself would become an "independence-wallah"—a champion of the cause of complete independence. And Nehru, leader of the Independence League was invited to become the youngest President at the Lahore session of the Congress.

Since that time any possibility of Nehru providing an alternative leadership was ruled out. He continued to talk and write as a leftist, he opposed many of Gandhi's basic ideas and current policies both openly and in private but never carried this implicit criticism to the logical expression of open and active opposition. He had surrendered himself to Gandhi, whose leadership became once more unchallenged, unassaillable. Later on, Gandhi had described the whole relationship succintly: "As for Jawaharlal, we know that neither of us can do without the other, for there is a heart union between us which no intellectual differences can break."

It was the success of this previous strategy of "heart union" which a decade later made Gandhi employ similar tactics in an attempt to bring under his control the tide of popular feeling for the left wing with its more radical policies, which would have found its most daring expression in the country through the personality of Bose.

Since the suspension of the civil disobedience movement in 1933 there had been open and widespread dissatisfaction with Gandhi's leadership. The most notable and organised manifestation of this tendency was the formation of the Congress Socialist Party, led by Jayaprakash Narayan in 1934. While in

Europe at that time Bose, without mincing words, wrote in his book "The Indian Struggle" that India's salvation would not be achieved under Gandhi's leadership and gave his own ideas for the fight for Indian freedom. When he came back to India in 1936 he was immediately arrested but was released again in late 1937. After that he paid a short visit to Europe and it was obvious that on his return he would plunge himself into Congress activities and would promote his left wing views. While still in Europe he was informed of his unanimous election as President of the Congress and it is known that it was Gandhi who was behind this move.

But as later events showed Bose was not to be won over by the feelings of personal gratitude towards Gandhi but preferred to act independently. "Ordinarily Mahatmaji's word is law to me but where principles are involved I sometimes feel unable to accept his advice or suggestion", he said.

Organizationally he wanted the Congress more closely tied with peasant and trade union movements; he was opposed to any kind of compromise with the British government and as the President of the Congress he started the National Planning Committee to prepare the plan for the development of Free India along modern lines, a plan quite alien to Gandhian concept. It must have been quite clear to Gandhi and his right wing friends that Bose was made of a different metal from Nehru and if he were to continue with another term of office in 1939 then his growing power and popularity would be further enhanced making increasingly difficult to dislodge him. Unless Gandhi's leadership were to be lost entirely, it would be necessary to exercise a timely check on his activities. Bose's victory in the Presidential election was unexpected. It showed clearly that the Congress machinery patiently built up by Gandhi had got out of his control and it was high time to put his foot down. It became necessary to play for the highest stakes in order to save the situation and Gandhi played by hinting that under the new circumstances he might have to quit the Congress. The implication was clear : "either choose me and my path or choose Bose". The nationalist movement in India had obviously reached the crossroads.

The time for Bose's departure for the Tripuri session of the Congress arrived; he insisted on attending although affected by a serious illness. I remember the evening when an ambulance came to our house, uniformed men carrying the stretcher upto his room on the first floor. The atmosphere in the house was tense; voices were hushed; nobody smiled; slowly he was carried down to the waiting vehicle. Outside a large crowd had gathered but there were no slogans, none of the usual manifestations of enthusiasm.

At the Tripuri Congress the previous year's mood of rejoicing was absent. My uncle had been too ill on arrival to make the short presidential address that he had prepared and his photograph acted for him in the Presidential procession. He was in favour of giving a six-month ultimatum to the British government on the question of the national demand for independence, as he expected that in the Autumn of 1939 a crisis would develop in Europe. Failing that, Congress should launch a civil disobedience movement. This however was not accepted.

But the most important resolution was moved by the right wing leader from Uttar Pradesh, Pandit Pant, saying that "in view of the fact that Mahatma Gandhi alone can lead Congress and the country to victory during such a crisis, the Congress regards it as imperative that the executive authority of the Congress should command his implicit confidence and request the President to nominate the Working Committee for the ensuing year in accorance with the wishes of Gandhiji". They clearly wanted the democratically elected President of the Congress to be divested of all real powers.

Gandhi himself had kept away from the conference. When somebody suggested that Gandhi would not have approved of this resolution, Rajagopalachari, who seconded the resolution, said, "I agree that he (Gandhi) does not want this resolution. But we want to reiterate his policy and programme. It is we who want and do actually stand for the principles and policy for which he stands. We accept his leadership". It was a clever manoeuvre to restore the control of the Congress machinery by playing upon the emotion of the assembly regarding Gandhi. Many people thought that Gandhi purposely kept away (by raising a side-issue at Rajkot) in order to give his followers a free hand to reassert his control over the Congress. The resolution was passed with a comfortable majority, with bewildered Congress Socialists abstaining in this vital power struggle between left and right within the Congress.

From Tripuri my uncle went to stay with another uncle of mine, Sudhir, at Jealgora for rest and treatment. We were told that Nehru came to see him there. In long and detailed discussion Bose made his last efforts to get Nehru, who all through had played a very ambiguous game with his leftist pretensions and Gandhian heart, on to his side. But without success.

After his recovery he returned to Calcutta. It was a hot summer night. The whole family in several cars went to Howrah station which was jammed with people. Fortunately, the train was to arrive on the central platform of the station where the cars could be brought in. So we stayed on in our car for fear of being stampeded by the jostling, restless crowd. From there we saw the ensuing tussle between a band party of Congress volunteers who were determined to play and the police who said it was not lawful to play the band inside the station. Soon the train slowly steamed up to the platform. The whole station reverberated with deafenning cries of greetings and slogans and the band burst forth triumphant. After a long wait we saw him carried away in an open car, literally drowned in garlands. For me, it was a tremendously moving experience. It was a wonderful thing, I thought, to be loved, almost worshipped by so many people.

In April 1939 the All India Congress Committee met at Wellington Square in Calcutta. The deadlock over the nomination of the new Working Committee had continued because Gandhi refused to co-operate and requested Bose to have a homogeneous leftist cabinet of his own choosing which he could not possibly do on the basis of the resolution passed at Tripuri.

Bose had two alternatives : either to yield to the pressure of the right wing and became a 'second Nehru' or to resign. We did not go to the meeting because the atmosphere there was so tense. There was a widespread feeling in Calcutta that there was a conspiracy against Bose to oust him and that generated a strong feeling of resentment towards the right wing leadership. We were told that uncle had a difficult time trying to control the fury of some of his hot-headed followers and in spite of his best efforts there were some nasty incidents. At this session he resigned from the preidency and formed a radical progressive platform, the Forward Bloc, within the Congress, with the idea of rallying all left wing forces under one banner. During this period a number of the left wing figures such as Jayaprakash Narayan, M. N. Roy, Sardar Sardul Singh Caveesher, Swami Sahajanand Saraswati became familiar to us as visitors to our house.

One evening a few months later we were at home and studying when we heard the shrill calling of the newspaper hawker. We listened intently because we had never such an outburst of frantic crying before. He came nearer. Now it was loud and clear : "Larhai suru ho giya !"—the war has started, "Germany attacks Poland !" We rushed down the stairs to buy a paper, and returned, reading the headlines in a state of high excitement. Six months ago at the Tripuri session of the Congress Bose had correctly predicted the advent of a big crisis. "This would be India's golden opportunity," he said. We were jubilant, full of the sense of imminent action, of world-shaking events.

But the right wing leadership was not eager to take advantage of the situation for moral considerations. Gandhi said : "We do not seek our independence out of Britain's ruin. That is not the way of non-violence". And Nehru was of the opinion that "the launching of a civil-disobedience campaign at a time when Britain is engaged in a life and death struggle would be an act derogatory to India's honour."

Immediately after Britain had declared war on Germany the Viceroy had announced India to be a belligerent and issued an ordinance containing the most stringent powers for the suppression of internal disorder. The Constitution of 1935 was suspended and all powers were concentrated in the hands of the Viceroy and in many parts of the country severe restrictions on personal liberty were imposed.

The struggle began between the right and left wing of Congress over the question of co-operation with Britain in her war effort. Bose took an openly anti-war policy and started preparations for a civil disobedience movement. It was because of his policy which had popular support, that the right wing leaders could not offer unconditional support to the war effort. Congress asked the British government to announce its war aims and declared that if India were granted freedom she would associate with Britain for mutual defence against aggression. But the Viceroy did not offer anything but Dominion Status at some future date. The left wing maintained a consistently anti-compromise policy. The right wing leaders obviously had infinite faith in a "change of heart" of even the arch-priest of British imperialism, Winston Churchill, the then Prime Minister of Britain. Churchill had repeatedly made his opinion on Indian freedom clear. "Sooner or later, you will have to crush Gandhi and Indian Congress and all they stand for," he said in 1930. Later on, he added, "We have no intention of casting away that most truly bright and precious jewel in the crown of the King, which more than all our dominions and dependencies constitutes the glory and strength of the British empire."

Yet the Congress leaders expected that this man would ultimately see things in a different light. And why not ? Had not he, the most stubborn and outspoken anti-Bolshevik in Britain, at a later stage rushed to Moscow to offer the hand of friendship to Stalin in their common struggle against Nazi Germany? For the security and independence of Britain everything was permissible Would not the same Churchill have agreed to an independent India, allied to Britain in a joint war effort, if it seemed that India's role in the war was to be seriously jeopardised by internal disorder and strife ?

But the Congress leaders completely ignored the basic realities of power politics. Churchill knew very well that in the hour of Britain's greatest need India was vitally necessary to her. As he had said "England, apart from her empire in India ceases forever to exist as a great power."

Looking back one cannot but help feeling that the right wing leaders were playing with the fate of millions of people in India without even an elementary understanding of the modern political game. With a whimsical prophet at its head, the right wing could explain away all these weaknesses with vague "moral" platitudes.

In Britain's most fateful hour Churchill proved to be her saviour; all credit to him for that. But for the Indian freedom fighters he was as deadly an enemy as ever, even when the freedom of Britain itself was seriously threatened, and he had a clear understanding of power politics. It is therefore not surprising that the British government did not take the right wing leaders seriously because of their weak-kneed and vacillating policies. The Congress offer was rejected. The British had no intention whatever of parting with power in India. They had no reason to do so. In 1945 Nehru wrote with heavy heart about the rejection of their offer: "They (the British) were bent on encouraging division and strengthening every medieval and reactionary element. They seemed to prefer civil war and the ruin of India to a relaxation of their imperialist control." What a profound discovery! Why should one expect an imperialist government to have any other intention? I do not criticize Churchill for what he was. He always put his ideas with vivid clarity and conviction. I blame the right wing leaders of the Congress for not having the political acumen to see the obvious.

Having being rejected by the British government, being under the continuous pressure of Bose and his followers, the right wing had no other alternative but to take some course of action. Great care was taken to see that the civil disobedience did not turn into a popular upheaval. A new technique—individual civil disobedience—was evolved. The leading Congress workers after having passed some kind of test, obtained permission from the Congress High Command to offer *satyagraha*. It started in October 1940. I was at that time at my sister's house in Jessore (now in Bangladesh) and saw this individual satyagraha. A well known Congress leader of the district notified the Police that he would offer satyagraha in the centre of the town at a specific time. His action was made known to the public as well. So we went to the place and saw that a large crowd had already gathered. There was also a police officer with a number of constables. The Congress leader with garlands around his neck and a Congress flag in his hand came walking forward. He shouted in a loud voice to the gathering multitude that they should not help the war effort. Immediately the police officer arrested him, putting him into a police van drove away. That was it!

What an anti-climax! I thought. Before the satyagraha had taken place the situation had been quite tense but somehow the garlanded shouting figure had only lessened the tension and the people began to drift away. It was a tame, pathetic affair.

In July 1940 my uncle had already been arrested for writing an article entitled "The Day of Reckoning" and also for delivering a speech at Mohammad Ali Park in Calcutta. He was not put up for trial for under the Defence of India Act it was not necessary. It was expected that during the rest of the war period he would be kept in prison. He had been in British custody eleven times since 1921 and felt that it would be "a gross political blunder to remain inactive in prison when history was being made elsewhere."

He explored all the legal methods to secure his release but none was effective. So he decided to send an ultimatum to the British government pointing out that there was no moral or legal justification for detaining him in prison and that if he were not released immediately he would fast unto death. He was determined to get out of prison, dead or alive. After seven days of fasting, his condition became worse and as the British government could not face the popular wrath that would have resulted if he had died in prison, they decided to release him with the idea of arresting him again when he had recovered. That was in November 1940.

By this time, we had left Calcutta for Dumka in Santhal Parganas. My uncle was at home only for forty days and created the highest political sensation in India by disappearing from the Elgin Road house in January 1941 although being watched closely by the secret police. For more than one full year complete mystery enveloped his disappearance. We did not know where or how he had gone although there was a great deal of speculation.

So it was, that by 1941, India had become a vast prison camp with all political activities either in prison or working underground. Civil disobedience continued without much enthusiasm and without any hope of substantial concessions from the British government. There was a lull. The country seemed blanketted in impotence and apathy. In a village in Santhal Parganas I saw starved and naked children and had smelt the stink of poverty and degradation and was born again into a new world where action was imperative; where to see and to do nothing was a sin against myself, and against mankind.

CHAPTER III

"In our time the destiny of man presents its meaning in political terms."—Thomas Mann.

But what could a boy of thirteen do? My mind was full of question. Why do these people suffer? How can the suffering be removed? Compared to them, why am I so fortunate? Is it a matter of fate or 'karma'? Or, is it the socio-economic system created by man, which can therefore be changed by men? One question led to another until I found I was asking fundamental questions which man has asked himself since the beginning of time. Who am I? From where did I come and to where shall I go? What is life and its purpose? Is it worth living? There seemed to be no end to my questioning but inevitably I returned to the original problem—the suffering of my countrymen and what was the part I must play in trying to solve it.

If the misery that I had seen in the village had come to me in an individualised form; if I had been moved, for instance, by the crying of Haradhan's younger sister, I should have known exactly what to do. I would have given some money to her mother. In fact, the normal reaction would seem to have been a philanthropic one, or the performance of some kind of social service to alleviate the situation to the best of my ability. Here I would have found satisfaction in seeing the concrete and positive results of my endeavour. But what of all those whom my limited efforts would never touch? I should be forever haunted by a million unknown sufferers in the hundreds of thousands of villages scattered beneath the pitiless Indian sun. They were as much part of my existence as those who were in my immediate environment.

To have discovered an answer or to have found an escape in the realm of philosophy or religion was another possibility. This path held a suitable attraction for me. I felt its compulsion in those persistent questionings in my mind leading to philosophical problems. In the religious and philosophical tradition in which I was brought up there are explanations for these problems and solutions as well. These millions of people suffer because in their previous birth they have committed sin. My favoured situation was due to the good work that I had done in my previous life. What I should be really concerned about was my salvation so that I might not be born into the world of suffering again—the world of "maya". But somehow this argument did not appeal to me because the misery that I had witnessed was very real and could not be wished away as an illusion. Moreover, this would have entailed a dissociation of myself from the original emotional experience which had triggered off this explosion of thought in the first place. It would have meant devoting my life to the search for Reality for purely selfish satisfaction.

But perhaps because the metaphysical propensities in my nature were weak, or rather because the sense of physical reality was more acute, I was dragged back to the world of suffering which imposed a feeling of responsibility and duty on me.

Finally, out of all my observation, reading and listening came the answer to my first urgent question. "Why do these people suffer? What can I do?" The solution seemed simple and straightforward. The basic cause of India's poverty was the British rule and exploitation of the country and its people. Until we had got rid of the oppressors no effective steps could be taken to remedy the situation. Therefore, all efforts had to be made so that India might be freed from the shackles of slavery. I think I came early and easily to this way of thinking because of the atmosphere of intense political activity in which I was brought up. Even today I have found no reason to think that it was an incorrect evaluation.

But political action as a solution is not always an attractive one. For an indefinite time the ills it seeks to overcome have to be tackled in an indirect way. Instead of offering food, medicine, or housing to poverty-stricken people the politicians at that time had nothing to hold out but more suffering in the struggle for independence and the distant hope of a better life. A politician's life seems comparatively cold and unfeeling; it is dominated by objective thought and calculation. But I was only a boy and these negative aspects of the political life did not deter me from thinking of politics as synonymous with patriotism and I wanted above all to be a patriot. I was determined to make, if necessary, the supreme sacrifice for the cause of Indian independence and find fulfillment in it.

I came across a letter which my uncle Subhas wrote to the government before undertaking his fast unto death in Calcutta prison just before his disappearance. This document provided all the justification I needed for my sacrificial mood.

"Though there may be no immediate, tangible gain, no sacrifice is ever futile," he said. "It is through suffering and sacrifice alone that a cause can flourish and prosper, and in every age and clime the eternal law prevails--'the blood of martyr is the seed of the church'."

The appeal in this political testament I took to my heart: "Forget not that the greatest curse for a man is to remain a slave. Forget not that the grossest crime is to compromise with injustice and wrong. Remember the eternal law—you must give life if you want to get it. And remember that the highest virtue is to battle against inequity, no matter what the cost may be."

I became passionately interested in the Indian political struggle, Now I faced a new problem—how to commit myself body and soul to this struggle?

We were in Santhal Parganas and my father was a government official and therefore the immediate circle of my family was non-political. In addition, I was painfully shy. In spite of my positive urge I used to find it very difficult to make new contacts. With the general quiet on the Indian political scene and with no political contacts I found no means of expressing my political enthusiasm and I became very restive. However, I joined the local library and started to read extensively. Everything interested me and a few years later when I first became a member of the then Imperial Library (now called National Library) in Calcutta. I decided to read systematically. In order to do this I started making a list of books I wanted to read, according to the subjects. Enthralled and excited about the possibility of knowing so much, I started making the list with the card index number of subjects under the heading 'A'. When I found that there were twentytwo subjects with the initial letter of 'A' in which I was interested, I gave up making the list of books!

Until this time I had not been a bad student, but now I completely lost interest in my studies. The text books we had to study contained nothing which helped me to arrive at answers to any of the questions which occupied my mind. In no time my school work deteriorated, much to my tutor's disgust. He admonished me with the warning that I should get nowhere in the world unless I studied harder. This left me unmoved because I did not want to get anywhere in the worldly life. It seemed that the pursuit of knowledge for purely personal gain would be the expression of a distorted sense of values.

I was caught between two realities; that of my own perception, understanding and convictions about the world around me; and the reality which absorbed all the energies and enthusiasm of those intelligent, loving, lovable and respectable people who led their lives, untouched by the poverty and suffering of large masses of people around them. Yet these people, my friends, my relations seemed normal. Was I then abnormal in my perception and evaluation? Yet I felt that I was right and they were wrong. So many of these normal people seemed to express an inexhaustible excitement over things which were so obviously trivial and insignificant. I did not want to become involved in their mad rush and yet struggling to stand apart from it, I felt a great loneliness as though I belonged to a different world. It was as though I spoke a language which had an entirely different meaning and I felt myself a stranger in my own land. In a letter I wrote at this time I tried to express something of this existentialist 'angst' about which I became intellectually acquainted many years later. "Sometimes I used to come across a line or two, perhaps written in a far away country or in the distant past, which I could understand and which brought temporary relief. Everything was temporary except unhappiness. I did not know how to tread the path I knew I must take. I took none to my trust. I dragged on with my fancies."

One of my fancies of that time was Death. Life it seemed was nothing more than a living death. Death would be a relief. But suicide did not appeal to me. I had acquired too much political sense for that. I wanted to die but in the freedom struggle and contribute my own donation of blood to water the tree of liberty.

During this time I found powerful support for my way of thinking from an unexpected quarter Rabindranath Tagore, for whom I had the highest regard as a poet and seer and who during the dark days of my uncle's struggle with the right wing, expressed his sympathy for him and ultimately greeted him as the leader of the people, died in August 1941. From his death bed he dictated his last message and among other things he said :

"The wheels of fate will some day compel the English to give up their Indian Empire. But what kind of India will they leave behind, what stark misery? When the stream of their centuries' administration runs dry at last, what a waste of mud and filth they will leave behind!

"Today we witness the perils which attend on the insolence of might; one day shall be borne out the full truth of what the sages have proclaimed : 'By unrighteousness man prospers, gains what appears desirable, conquer enemies, but perishes at the root.' "

I wanted to nourish the root even if the whole world looked at me with scorn and contempt.

CHAPTER IV

"We shall either free India or die in the attempt."
—Mahatma Gandhi.

Suddenly at the end of 1941 came the bombshell. Japan attacked Pearl Harbour.

From our younger days we had a great admiration and fascination for Japan. She stood, in the farthest corner of the Asian continent, a living contradiction of the widely-held belief that unless an Asian country was under the domination of the West, she could not make progress as a modern and industrial nation. That Japan had once inflicted a crushing defeat on Russia, a western power, was a fact which kindled our racial confidence. Having been under British rule for nearly two centuries we sought in every possible way to prove the worth of our own country and continent. We did this in two ways; first by glorifying our past. When West Europeans lived like barbarians, we said, the Indians had not only established a highly developed civilization but also had evolved the subtlest forms of metaphysics. But the wheel of history does not stand still; it turns. Though now we might be down, one day we would rise again and there was every reason to believe that day was not far off.

Secondly, we found inspiration in the present achievements of Japan freed from western domination, and derived negative satisfaction from any humiliation inflicted on the western imperialist powers. We knew there were only two countries in the world who could do this, Japan and Germany.

Before the war I had a strong feeling of sympathy for Germany because of the humiliation she had suffered after the first world war. We belonged to the same camp of defeated and humiliated peoples. At the same time we had great admiration for her scientific and technological progress. When the war began in Europe my feelings were mixed. I overjoyed by the defeat of British and French arms but my sympathy went out to those small nations which were crushed under the Nazi jackboot. But Germany was far away; Russia, strangely enough, had no attraction for the popular imagination before the second world war. But Japan, on the other hand, engaged all our enthusiastic attention when she entered the war.

In three short months after the attack on Pearl Harbour in December 1941, the whole Asian scene was transformed. The first blow to British prestige was the sinking of the 'unsinkable' "Prince of Wales". Then the impregnable fortress of Singapore failed to withstand the Japanese attack and fell on the 15th February 1942. The mighty British empire seemed to be collapsing like a house of cards. Masses of Indians started pouring into India from Burma. The war seemed no longer remote; it was next door and might soon reach India itself. The whole country was electrified and it was obvious that if the Japanese wanted to invade our country the British government was in no position to defend it. It was common knowledge that in case of a Japanese attack the British would retreat from Assam and Bengal and try to take up defensive positions in the hills of Chhotanagpur in Bihar. Everyone was discussing with apprehension the possibility of a Japanese attack from the air on the cities of Calcutta and Madras.

In January 1942 the Congress Working Committee met and passed a resolution offering to co-operate in the war effort again, but Gandhi could not reconcile himself with supporting a violent war and differences consequently developed between him and other right wing leaders on this issue.

On the 7th of March Rangoon fell and four days later Winston Churchill was forced to make some conciliatory moves and announced that Sir Stafford Cripps would visit India on behalf of the British War Cabinet. From the Indian Nationalist point of view this was an excellent choice. Cripps was considered to be one of the most radically-minded within the British Labour Party. He was an avowed champion of Indian independence and great hopes were placed upon his visit. But to everyone's disappointment what was offered was far more dangerous than any previous plan. He brought the promise of Dominion Status after the war ended in return for present cooperation. The proposal gave the right to the provinces not to join the Indian Union unless they wished. The same right of non-accession was given to six hundred and odd of the princely states. In the provinces the election for the constitution-making body was to be on the basis of the existing separate religious electorate; while the feudal rulers of the Indian states would nominate (there was to be no election) their own representatives according to the size of their population. It was a systematic effort to dismember India and to create as many divisions as possible.

Why did the British government adopt such a retrograde attitude at the hour of her greatest peril, when the very existence of her empire was threatened? It confirmed in the mind of every Indian how deep were the roots of imperialist tradition in Britain. But what shocked us most was that one of the most left wing members of British Labour movement was prepared to do this job.

It might be argued that at that time Britain was facing almost single-handed the Nazi threat to her freedom. Only a united Britain could face this grave challenge and therefore the British Labour movement could not have divided the nation on the side-issue of Indian independence. Therefore, perhaps with some reservations, Churchill's lead had to be accepted on all major policies, including that of Indian independence. But we were not interested in all the subtleties of British internal politics. We were the largest nation in the world under foreign colonial rule and were, so to speak, the kingpin of all the struggles of the colonial peoples for freedom and independence. The Allied powers had declared that they were fighting for the preservation of freedom and democracy and yet, we who wanted freedom and democracy were denied it. Churchill made it very clear that the Atlantic Charter was not meant for the Indians and other such inferior peoples. The Charter was meant for the white people only. Was it, therefore, surprising that the Indians were not interested in the "crusade" and wanted to assert their own right to freedom?

The expectation that Sir Stafford Cripps could bring something better was a mistaken one. The British Labour movement, although calling itself Socialist, had never taken a genuinely socialist line on imperial questions. The key method of British Labourites had been "gradualism" in every sphere and it was applied to the British empire as well. This policy was based on three basic assumptions; that British imperialism had been beneficial for the people it had governed; that there should be gradual introduction of self-governing institutions and that should ultimately lead to self-government at the "proper time". This had been the proclaimed policy of the British government since 1858 when it was clearly stated in Queen Victoria's proclamation. This, combined with the attempts to create as many divisions as possible among the ruled, had been the traditional policy of British imperialism, whoever was in power: Tories, Liberals or Labour. There were some differences in the Labour movement about the pace of development but these differences existed in the Conservative and Liberal Parties as well. There had been, for instance, within the British Labour movement a vocal minority who stood clearly for the Indian independence at the earliest possible moment. But the upholders of this policy were few and their influence was limited.

The British empire was the vested interest of the whole British people from which all sections of the population, from the highest to the lowest, benefitted. The British Labour movement was aware of this fact and having the interest of the British people at heart, never contemplated giving a real body-blow to the empire thereby antagonising British public opinion. After the arrival of Sir Stafford Cripps, any lingering expectations which still existed in some quarters in India, that the British Labour movement would try to champion the cause of Indian independence were completely shattered. It was proved, if any further proof were required, that the British Labour movement was as much a part of British imperialist establishment as the Conservatives. During this period Gandhi observed that the Labour Party and *Daily Herald* excelled every one else in Britain in abusing Congress. About Sir Stafford Cripps he said: "Sir Stafford in a very good man but he has entered a bad machinery, British imperialism. He hopes to improve that machinery but in the end it is the machinery that will get the better of him. The fact is, that Sir Stafford, having become a part of the imperial machinery consciously partook of its quality. Such is its strength."

There was no possibility for negotiation on the Cripps proposal because it had to be accepted or rejected as a whole. Regarding the dangerous possibilities of balkanisation of India that was inherent in the Cripps proposal the Congress Working Committee said in a resolution: "Congress has been wedded to Indian freedom and unity and any break in that unity, specially in the modern world when people's minds inevitably think in terms of ever larger federations, would be injurious to all concerned and exceedingly painful to contemplate".

Although the Congress rejected the proposal it still wanted to co-operate in the war effort. The proposal had made it clear that the defence of India must remain the sole charge of the British government. The right wing, inspired by Jawaharlal Nehru, was very keen to arrive at a compromise. But they knew that the Indian people would not stomach a compromise beyond certain limits. So they insisted that there should be an Indian Defence member in the Viceroy's Executive Council because during war time everything is subjected to the needs of defence. If they had no substantial say in that sphere then the participation in the government would not amount to anything. The British government agreed and said that the Indian Defence Minister would look after canteens, stationery and printing, social arrangements for foreign visitors and other minor affairs. This was ludicrous, but the leaders still hoped that something might come out of it. The British government was firm that there would be only additions to the existing Executive Council, made up from British stooges, coopted from different political parties. All powers as before would be concentrated in the hands of the Viceroy both in theory and in practice. The British government had not made even the slightest concession since its previous offer eighteen months ago, which Congress had then rejected.

In spite of the over-eagerness of the right wing leaders to reach a settlement, the British government did not give them the opportunity, even though the Congress leaders had compromised every fundamental stand which they had taken for years. They knew that such was the mood in the country that if they had accepted the British proposals as they stood, they would be denounced. In fact, later on when it was publicly known to what extent the leaders had gone to make compromises, there was a wide-spread outcry.

Moulana Abul Kalam Azad, the then Congress President, in his letter to Sir Stafford Cripps wrote : "But, unhappily, even in this grave hour of peril the British government is unable to give up its wrecking policy. We are driven to the conclusion that it attaches more importance to holding on to its rule in India as long as it can and promoting discord and disruption here with that end in view, than to an effective defence of India against the aggression and invasion that overhang us."

Cripps made his farewell address to the Indian people on the 11th of April and then left India a disappointed man.

Just before the arrival of Sir Stafford Cripps in India, however, the whole country was stunned by the news in the headlines of every paper that my uncle had been killed in an air crash while flying from South East Asia to Japan. Since January 1941 there had been no news of him and this was a grievous blow. Gandhi sent a condolence message to my grandmother.

But soon after this, curious rumours were abroad that he had been heard speaking from an unknown radio station. Since we had no radio at that time we had no means of verifying for ourselves whether this development was true or false. In addition, to be found listening to the Axis radio (for it was widely held that broadcasts must either be from Japanese-occupied South East Asia, or Japan or Germany) was a punishable offence.

One day however a family friend came to visit us with the news that he had been able to pick up a station on which the speaker had introduced himself as Subhas Chandra Bose. Since he had never heard Bose speak before he was unable to testify whether or not it was his actual voice but suggested that we go and judge for ourselves. Elated, we went to his house on the following evening when a broadcast was scheduled to take place. All the doors and windows were closed and the radio was switched on. We waited in great suspense as the Azad Hind Radio (Free India Radio) repeatedly announced, while giving the news in Indian languages and in English, that my uncle would shortly be heard speaking on the same wave-length. There was silence. Then the voice came : "This is Subhas Chandra Bose speaking..." It was his voice and we were beside ourselves with joy. On very few occasions in my life have I experienced such overwhelming happiness. He gave an incisive analysis of the prevailing situation in India and the world outside, and explained why the Cripps proposals must firmly be rejected. Then he concluded with a stirring call for action against British imperialism. At a later date he made a special broadcast to Sir Stafford Cripps himself whom he had known personally.

Much speculation was made as to the source of the broadcasts. The opinion generally held was that they came from South East Asia though it was actually known later that they were made in Germany.

After the failure of Cripps Mission there was great suspense in the country. It was not only the Congress but every single political party and group which rejected this proposal. But in the British Parliament it was upon Gandhi's shoulders that the chief blame for the failure of the mission was placed. Gandhi had aptly called the offer a post-dated cheque on a crumbling bank. In India the whole episode was considered to be a propaganda move to impress American public opinion, which was sympathetic towards Indian freedom.

Soon afterwards the All India Congress Committee met to approve the rejection of Cripps proposal. In the absence of a compromise with Britain they decided that there was no question of actively fighting on the side of Britain against the Japanese. But in case of Japanese invasion the Congress decided to offer non-violent non-co-operation.

Gandhi did not attend the meeting but he sent a draft resolution in which he said : "Britain is incapable of defending India... Japan's quarrel is not with India. She is warring against the British Empire. If India were freed, her first step would probably be to negotiate with Japan. The Congress is of opinion that if the British withdraw from India, India would be able to defend herself in the event of Japanese or any other aggressors attacking India." The draft resolution assured the Japanese government and people that India bore no enmity towards Japan.

Nehru strongly criticised the draft saying : "The whole background of the draft is one which will inevitably make the whole world think we are passively linking up with the Axis powers." He submitted his own draft which was finally accepted. Although the Nehru resolution was adopted there was no doubt that the sentiments expressed by Gandhi had widespread support in the country. Nehru was of the opinion that even without a compromise India should fight alongside Britain against

Fascism. This was the line that the Indian Communists had adopted after the German attack on the Soviet Union in June, 1941. But this policy had neither the support of Gandhi, nor of the right and left wing of the Congress, nor of the general public. It was obvious that the interests of Indian nationalism and British imperialism were totally different and the clash between them was drawing nearer. The Congress resolution had noted that there was "a rapid and widespread increase of ill-will against Britain and a growing satisfaction at the success of Japanese arms."

During the Cripps negotiations large number of people were still in prison. Three members of our family, uncle Sarat, cousin Dwijen and brother Aurobindo were languishing behind bars in places far away from home. From May 1942 the leaders of the right wing of the Congress were being picked up and it was obvious that the British government wanted to completely remove all the opposition forces from the scene. This caused widespread resentment. Gandhi wrote a number of articles in "Harijan", his weekly paper. He said that the only way to meet the situation was by the recognition of Indian freedom and for a free India to meet aggression with the co-operation of the Allied nations. If the British government did not accept this course then action must be taken to challenge the existing system. There should not be submission to Britain's autocratic and repressive rule, the continuance of which would break the spirit of India. While he talked of action he did not define what that action would be. He clung to the belief that a settlement with the British government was still possible.

While the Congress leaders fumbled, the mood of the country changed. There was restlessness and impatience at the speed at which the Congress leaders moved. By that time my uncle's broadcasts were reaching a wide audience. There was no doubt that they were having a marked effect on an influential section of the public.

The All India Congress Committee met at the historic session in Bombay in August 1942 to consider the famous "Quit India" resolution which declared that Britain's rule in India must end immediately and Gandhi in an inspiring speech said : "Every one of you should, from this moment onwards, consider yourself a free man or woman, and act as if you are free and are no longer under the heels of imperialism. It is not a make-believe that I am suggesting you. It is the very essence of freedom. The bond of the slave is snapped the moment he considers himself to be a free being."

His final message was "Here is a *mantra,* a short one, that I give you. You may imprint it on your hearts and let every breath give expression to it. The mantra is : Do or Die : We shall either free India or die in the attempt. We shall not live to see the perpetuation of our slavery."

The resolution was passed on the late evening of 8th August, with only the Communists and a few followers of Rajagopalachari opposing. Within a few hours all the leaders, including Gandhi and Nehru, were arrested.

The Government of India explained its stand in a statement. The acceptance of the Congress demand, it said, would mean not only the betrayal of "their responsibilities to the people of India" but must also "mean betrayal of the allies, whether in or outside India, the betrayal in particular of Russia and China, the betrayal of those ideals to which so much support has been given and is being given today from *the true heart and mind of India.*" (Italics mine). In history one rarely finds a parallel to such stupendous hypocrisy.

After the resolution was passed both Gandhi and Moulana Azad, the Congress President, declared that their next step would be to appeal to the Viceroy and the heads of allied nations for an honourable settlement. This appeal would be that the recognition of India's freedom would also help the cause of the Allied nations in their struggle against the Axis powers. But no time was given either to do this, or to organise and conduct the struggle. The news of the arrest of the leaders flashed across the country like a wildfire and was met with widespread anger. Being deprived of the leaders both at national and local levels and without any clear-cut directives, the people began to act upon their own initiative and express their resentment through demonstrations before the government buildings, by organising protest meetings and by resorting to strikes. On 10th August, the government declared the Congress to be an unlawful association, making it clear that anybody who assisted in its operation would be prosecuted under the Criminal Law Amendment Act. The closing of shops and restaurants was forbidden by new Defence of India Act rules. There was complete suppression of all news of disturbances.

I followed the whole development with growing interest. When finally the "Quit India" resolution was passed and Gandhi gave his inspiring call of "Do or Die", I knew that the time that I had been waiting for had come at last. However, due to the complete suppression of news, one could not have known that India was passing through the biggest convulsions in the history of her struggle for freedom since the first war of independence of 1857. The only news that we obtained was from Free India Radio in Saigon and from the stories of travellers. I still remember one evening when I heard over the radio that a peaceful demonstration at Kanpur was fired and three persons were killed. I could not go on listening to the radio any more. I walked out of the room in furious rage. I felt like Herzen: "Such minutes deserve ten years of hate and a life-time of vengeance." But it was an impotent rage. I wished I had a gun to fight and to die fighting. But there was no gun.

News had reached us from Calcutta that there were widespread disturbances. As elsewhere it was the students who had taken the leading part. I decided to join the movement at the earliest possible moment. I was then thirteen and half years old.

Henceforward, my only thought was how I could escape to Calcutta unnoticed. Upto that time I had never travelled alone and in order to reach Calcutta one had to travel about forty miles in a bus from Dumka to Rampurhat. From there one had to take the train to Calcutta, about 130 miles away. I discovered that there were two buses, one in the morning and the other at night and I decided that I would catch the evening bus while pretending to go for a walk. When I did not return home in time I knew my parents would send somebody to the town to find me, but even if they had suspected that I had run away, I imagined that by the time our bus reached Rampurhat, my train would be leaving and I should be out of reach. It seemed to be a sound plan.

During this time uncle was speaking regularly over the radio giving instructions on how to conduct the struggle. One of the methods he had suggested, I remember, was travelling the government-owned trains without paying any money. So I decided that my defiance of the government would start as soon as I arrived at Rampurhat when I would board the train without a ticket. They might arrest me and put me in prison. They would impose a fine which I would not pay and I would undergo a few days imprisonment. But I would soon be released and then I would board the train again. Finally I would reach Calcutta in triumph, join one of the demonstrations, get lathi-charged, tear-gased, charged at by the Mounted Police, or be arrested or shot. Anything was good for me because I had resolved to "Do or Die."

As I could not possibly go by private bus without paying, I collected a little sum of money and some extra pocket money for food. I decided I must take at least a change of shorts and a clean shirt and a towel rolled up in a newspaper. If I was to die I must die clean!

The fact that I would leave home, never to return, without telling anybody aroused in me some strong sentimental feelings but they were soon swept away by other more violent emotions. I had only one over-riding desire — to be killed. Nothing short of that would satisfy me. I never imagined the situation in which I might be shot in the foot or just be maimed for life. It was to be death and glory, or nothing.

Just before I was to leave, I yielded to sentiment. I could not conceal my vast secret from my closest friend — my elder brother, Partho. I made him promise three times with great solemnity that he would not divulge the secret that I was about to tell him. Three times he promised. Then I gave my news that I would be leaving secretly to join the freedom movement.

The next day dawned peacefully enough, with no sign that it was a day of momentous action. I had planned that after taking afternoon refreshment I would slip off unnoticed. I had packed my things in a newspaper and began to look for an opportunity to escape. All the time it seemed that I was being obstructed; always there was someone talking or watching, barring the way. In the end I came to the conclusion that if I did not leave almost immediately there would be no hope of catching the bus. The house we lived in at that time was built on the bungalow design, with a large compound surrounded by hedges. I decided to leave from the back of the house. When I was nearing the hedge my eldest brother, Ranjit called me. I felt that I must start running but I realised the fruitlessness of such effort, because I knew I would be caught in no time. So I turned and asked him in as nonchalant manner as possible: "What it is?"

"Where are you going " he asked.

"For a walk."

"What is it in your hand?"

By that time I knew that Partho had betrayed my trust and had informed my family about my intentions. So the only way was for me to fight my way out.

"My clothes", I answered.

"Why are you carrying them?"

"Because I am going to Calcutta."

"What for?"

"To join the movement."

"To join the movement? What do you understand of politics that you want to join the movement?"

"I know nothing about politics. But this much I know that this is the time to join the movement because Gandhiji says so; uncle says so."

"Young boys do not go to join the movement."

"Those who understand, can! I do."

"Stop talking in that arrogant tone." He was losing his temper.

I lost my temper too. "Who has asked you to interfere in my affairs," I demanded.

By that time most of the family had gathered around to see what the trouble was. My mother rebuked me, saying that one should not speak like that to elder. "I do not care for elders", I cried.

Ranjit came back to politics. "Do you know how many groups there are in the nationalist movement? Do you know that they often hate each other more than they hate the British? If you do not belong to any of the groups then nobody will care for you."

I said: "I do not want them to care for me. I want to do my duty."

The argument went on in circles. It became clear that I should not be able to catch the bus about which I had been dreaming for days. Our house was the last one on the road to

Rampurhat. I had even thought when the bus carrying me was approaching the house I would pretend that I was tying my shoe lace and duck so that if anybody stood in our house near the road they would not be able to see me. While arguing I heard the sound of the bus approaching. Soon it would pass by and I knew everything was lost. I stopped the argument, rushed to our study, banged the door and started crying. I had never felt so utterly, utterly helpless. A fire was burning inside me which urged me to make the greatest sacrifice that anyone can make—to give my life in the cause of independence, and here I was sobbing in the prison of my house.

Evening drew on. It was time to study. I was asked to open the door which I had bolted from inside but I did not reply. I sat there in the darkness. After sometime the dinner gong went. My mother decided to leave me alone until I had recovered; nobody came to call me for dinner. When I was sure everybody was in the dining room I slipped out of the study and surreptitiously went to bed. I knew from now on I should be kept under strict surveillance, unable to make any further plans for escape. I felt condemned to a living death. Henceforward I lived in the house like a stranger. I did not talk to anybody unless it was absolutely necessary. I was very angry with my brother, who tried to befriend me but I firmly rejected him. My attitude towards everybody changed; I considered them my enemies because they had deprived me of my highest fulfillment.

I had one friend the Alsatian, Frieda. I loved her dearly. If I were sitting somewhere alone, she would not leave me. She would bring a ball or a stone and place it before my feet. If I took no notice she would scratch me or bark, begging me to throw so that she could enjoy her little game. At first I felt estranged from her as well, but she would not leave me, and she looked so happy if I did something for her. She continued to love me in spite of my madness. I could not help loving her in return. I used to take her on my long, lonely walks. Besides books, she remained my only solace. But Frieda did not understand me. I could not tell her my thoughts.

Meanwhile events in India followed one another with lighting speed. Suddenly British tommies poured into our little town in large convoys. We heard that they had come to crush a big rebellion of the Santhals in the hilly areas. As Churchill said later: "The disturbances were crushed with all the weight of the government." According to the government, there was firing on unarmed demonstrators on 538 occasions, killing 1,028 and wounding 3,200. Nationalist circles consider it to be a gross underestimate. According to their calculation 10,000 people were killed. Every conceivable method of brutal suppression was adopted: villages were burnt, women were raped, prisoners were tortured, collective fines were imposed and there was even machine gunning of the people from lowflying aircrafts. It was clear that the British were capable of as much brutality as the Nazis if there was a real challenge to their authority. After the August Revolution of 1942 the so-called moral superiority of British imperialism was completely exposed.*

The Congress Socialists and the Forward Blockist, not too much encumbered with the theories of non-violence, played a valiant role in the struggle. There were massive strikes and parallel governments were formed in some parts of the country. But ultimately the military might of the British government brought the situation under control, although sporadic action continued here and there.

I was thoroughly ashamed and angry with the Indians in the police and military services who helped to suppress the revolt. It became obvious that all the "non-violent" strength of the Congress would not be able to remove British power from India unless there was a major defection in the British Army and police.

Another important fact was that, knowing that the nationalist forces had adopted violent tactics on an extensive scale, Gandhi did not call off the struggle as he had done on a previous occasion in 1921.

In February 1943 (at the age of 74) Gandhi undertook a 21-day fast in prison. The whole country was roused again and there was a widespread outcry for his release. I decided to fast

* In the British Parliament Churchill was supported by Attlee and the Labour Party. Only Bevan had protested: "Now in the name of Labour and Socialism he (Attlee) has underwritten one of the blackest documents which imperialist bigotry ever devised—Mr. Churchill's India—effusion." (Tribune 2.10.42).

for twenty four hours in sympathy. At one stage he was on the verge of death and if he had died in prison there would no doubt have been another convulsion. However, he survived. The nationalist forces inside the country were exhausted thereafter. Full of frustration at being unable to find expression for all the fire inside me, my attention was turned away from the situation in India, to events in the larger world outside.

CHAPTER V

"There is no power on earth which can keep India enslaved."
—Subhas Chandra Bose.

It was not until late 1942 that the details of my uncle's dramatic stage to Germany in 1941 became known to me. He was at that time broadcasting regularly from Berlin, and my sister, Ila who, among others in the family had assisted in his escape, gave the main outline of the most romantic and thrilling escape story of modern India.

After he has been released on parole by the British government, at the time of his fast unto death in November 1940, he returned to our Elgin Road house. After a few days he announced that he would not receive visitors as he was going to devote his time to meditation. This was not in itself a particularly surprising thing, as from his younger days he had a religious bent of mind. Only my brother Aurobindo Bose was allowed to go into his room once a day. None knew that behind the screen of privacy he had begun to grow a beard.

Then one night in the middle of January 1941 a car drew up in the dark. The driver was my cousin Sisir Bose. Afterwards it left carrying a passenger, a bearded Muslim from the north western part of the country in traditional dress. It drove past the plain clothes police who kept watch on the house day and night, and away out on the Grand Trunk Road, leaving Calcutta for Gomoh, about 210 miles away. Speeding through the night they arrive there hours later. The Muslim, now to be known as Mia Ziauddin, caught the train to Peshawar.

From Peshawar, accompanied by Bhagat Ram, now travelling under the alias Rehmat Khan, he began the hazardous journey to Kabul. Bhagat Ram belonged to the Kirti Kisan Party (Workers' and Peasants' Party) of the Punjab, with pronounced Communist leanings. They travelled through the barren mountainous region, while avoiding the main road between Peshawar and Kabul in order to avoid Indo-Afghan border post. Travelling in bitterly cold weather they walked through the lawless tribal areas in between the north west Frontier Province and

Afghanistan. Knowing neither the local language, Pushtu or Persian, Bose pretended to be deaf and dumb. After three days they reached the main road to Kabul at a spot far inside Afghanistan, where it was expected that no one would enquire for their non-existent passports.

In Kabul Bose attempted to contact the Russian ambassador in order to be able to travel to the Soviet Union, but without success. Meanwhile the Afghan C.I.D. were beginning to display a rather too much interest in the two strange travellers in the lorry drivers' inn. Back in Calcutta on the 26th of January, the very day that he was to have been tried for sedition, an announcement was made from our house (nearly two weeks after he had actually left) that he had disappeared from his room. The entire police force there was thrown into a ferment. Our house was invaded and searched from top to bottom and Aurobindo was arrested for interrogation. But the police did not get any clue from that quarter.

Knowing that the search for him would be intensified not only in India but also in neighbouring countries, Bose took shelter in the house of an Indian, Uttam Chand. Having failed to contact the Russians and knowing that he could not stay on indefinitely in Kabul, he managed to get in touch with the Italian Embassy and with their help travelled through the Soviet Union, disguised this time as an Italian and carrying an Italian passport in the name of Orlando Massotta. He travelled from Kabul to Samarkand by road and then took a train to Moscow, from where he boarded a plane for Berlin.

Back in India all border posts were under close observation and the police in every part of the country were put on the alert. But it was all too late. The escape plan had been flawless. With a face known to every man, woman and child, he yet managed to cross the whole breadth of the country undetected. By the time the police were awakened to the situation he had slipped through their net and passed beyond their reach.

Once in Europe he organised the Free India Legion from the Indian prisoners of war captured by the Germans and Italians in various campaigns and a sprinkling of volunteers from Indians living in Europe, and from the beginning of 1942 he began regular broadcasts. But when South East Asia was occupied by Japanese forces he decided to make an effort to reach Japan.

So it was, that in February 1943 he commenced the long and dangerous journey from Kiel, by German and then by Japanese submarine to Sumatra, where he took a plane to Tokyo. The whole journey took over four months.

In August 1943 he assumed the command of the Indian National Army which had already been organized in East Asia under the leadership of the late Rashbehari Bose and General Mohan Singh soon after the surrender of the British forces in 1942. A complete reorganization of the whole Indian national movement there was set on foot and in October the Provisional Government of Azad Hind (Free India) was proclaimed in Singapore, once the citadel of British imperialism. We had followed the whole development of the Azad Hind movement through regular broadcasts; it was clear to us that the main burden of India's freedom struggle now lay with the Indians outside India, and the momentous broadcast announcing the existence, after nearly two hundred years of slavery, of our own government brought tears of joy and elation to our eyes. The news, however, was suppressed by the British in India and later only became known to the people through the revelations of the Indian communist press which branded the Azad Hind Government a Japanese puppet regime.

Two days later, on October 23rd the Azad Hind Government declared war on British and the USA. This was a signal for the renewal of the armed struggle for India's freedom, by means which, as Bose said, were to be complementary to Gandhi's non-violent struggle inside the country. Breathlessly I waited for some dramatic developments, having given up hope of any decisive nationalist action inside the country until the end of the war.

It was a Sunday afternoon in December 1943. We had had lunch and I was studying when suddenly I heard far away the wailing of an air-raid siren. I rushed out onto the verandah where some of the family were sitting in winter sun.

"Did you hear the siren?" I demanded urgently.

They looked at me blankly. "You must be dreaming."

They ignored me and went on talking placidly. Then suddenly the air was split by the frantic screaming of the siren near to our house. Everyone leapt to their feet. We stood transfixed, wondering what to do next. Then came shouts telling everyone to come down to the ground flour immediately.

Against all the rules we went out into the road. The siren had stopped its persistent clamour. It was suddenly very quiet. We looked up at the bright azure sky. Nothing. Then came the sound of anti-aircraft guns firing; far up in the clear blue sky the salvoes exploided into little puffs of white smoke and then like silver swans, their plumage shinning in the sun, came a formation of Japanese planes. Undeterred by the attack from the ground they came steadily on. Form across the road the air raid warden yelled at us to take cover but we were hypnotised by the sight and dit not move. The planes looked beautiful, harmless and remote, and now passed over our heads towards the east and out of our range of vision. Then a second formation followed the first and like the others pursued an intrepid path through the furious ack-ack barrage. It seemed impossible that they would all escape and we expected to see at any moment a burning wreckage falling out of the sky on to the city below, but none were hit and soon they followed the others out of sight.

We wanted to go into the town to see whether there had been any bombs dropped but our elders feared the planes might return, and we had to be satisfied with climbing up to the roof, from where we could see black smoke arising from the south west side of Calcutta. Rumours spread like wildfire; we heard that injured people had been brought to a nearby hospital, so we went to see. Already a crowd of anxious bystanders had assembled. From passers by we gathered that a big American convoy of ships had arrived the previous day and consequently it was the docks which had been the only target for the air attack. A number of people had been killed and injured. The following day when we went down to the river, we found ships lying like wounded whales, their sides shattered and broken.

This was my first and last experience of air-raid in the second world war. Calcutta was the only major city to be bombed but on this occasion the fact that the residential areas had not been attacked at all appeared to indicate Japanese good will towards the Indian people. This bombing seemed to presage future events, for it seemed to us that the declaration of war by the Provisional Government woud be no idle threat, but would ultimately mean an attack on India itself. Suspense hung like thundercloud over the whole country.

In January 1944 the Azad Hind Government was moved to Rangoon from Singapore and in February an offensive was launched by the Japanese in Arakan which gained some spectacular success in bringing the fighting nearer to the Indian border.

However, the major attack began in the north in the second week of March, its aim being the capture of Imphal, the capital of Manipur. On March 19 the INA and Japanese forces crossed the Indian border and the tri-colour national flag was hoisted on Indian soil. Two days later, Tojo, the Japanese Premier declared that the Provisional Government of Azad Hind would be responsible for the administration of occupied Indian territory. The tide, it seemed, had turned.

Standing on the threshold of such tremendous events, the thoughts of my impending matriculation examination seemed of little importance, and I appeared in a state of complete unpreparedness. In spite of this, however, I managed to pass in all subjects, except mathematics, where I produced a miserable result. This held me up and made me even less enthusiastic about school studies.

Meanwhile on the 21st April Kohima fell. This was not announced by the British because Kohima was previously proclaimed as impregnable. The next target was Imphal. If this could have been captured before the rains came the operation would have been completely successful. After that it would be impossible for the Allied forces to hold back the INA and Japanese forces from the plains of Assam and Bengal. But although the combined armies came within a few miles of Imphal they failed to capture it, and they were overtaken by the onset of the monsoon. Communication through the hills and forests of northern Burma was completely disrupted and the campaign had to be formally suspended. By August it was clear that disaster had completely overtaken the invaders. The opportunity to occupy northern India was lost for ever, and the glow of hope which had lit up the beginning of 1944 had faded by the end of the year.

During the Imphal campaign Bose had made a proclamation in which he had stated "the Provisional Government of Azad

Hind is the only lawful government of the Indian people. The Provisional Government calls upon the Indian people to render all assistance and co-operation to the Indian National Army and to the civilian official appointed by the Provisional Government." Now although these events were happening in far-away places I had no doubt where my duty lay. If any opportunity arose for me to help the INA I knew that I should unhesitatingly do so and before long I became involved in a cloak-and-dagger situation which satisfied all my youthful sense of adventure.

It so happened during the summer of 1944 that brother-in-law Haridas Mitra came to our Elgin Road house one afternoon and asked me whether I would like to go with him in his car where there was a man who had been sent by my uncle from East Asia for intelligence and sabotage activities. I was thrilled and eagerly followed him to the waiting vehicle. Sitting in the front seat was a stranger wearing dark glasses.

Now during this period our family often found itself in an extremely awkward predicament. A number of people arrived claiming to belong to the INA, saying that they needed help in order to carry out specific instructions given to them. It was very difficult to check their identity and, in addition, we were well aware that the British were sending their own agents with similar stories in order to test our reactions. In fact, to help such people was a perilous venture. Anyone suspected of having dealings with any representative of the INA would be liable to prosecution; a secret trial with no real defence and with the maximum penalty of death would be the end of the story.

On the other hand, to refuse help to genuine INA agents would seem deplorable and on this occasion Haridas was convinced that the report given to him by the latest arrival was a bona fide one. According to him, four of the INA group had landed on the Orissa coast from a Japanese submarine. They had failed to contact the persons they had wanted to in India since they were all either in prison or working in the underground. The youngest one of the group, had, in a mood of desperation and frustration, done what had been absolutely forbidden by my uncle. He had made his way to the Elgin Road house, although it was at that time being closely watched night and day by the police. Here he accidentally met Haridas when he was leaving, and when convinced that Haridas was a member of the family he gave him his identity and sought his assistance.

So it came about that Haridas entered upon an adventure which almost cost his life. The group, two of whom met in Calcutta, possessed their own transmitter by which they used to send regular information to INA headquarters in Burma. This was kept first of all at Haridas' house in the city area of South Calcutta, but this was too dangerous a place because the military police vans fitted with detectors went on regular rounds searching for any kind of illegal radio transmitters. They therefore moved to the outskirts of the city and for some months they were able to continue their activities without any interruption. I remember once thinking to myself as I walked along Lake Road with one of the agents (both of whom are now respectable and respected members of society!) that at any moment we might be leapt upon by the police. In my youthful fantasies I imagined myself dragged off to prison and thrown into a dark and lonely cell where after many days of interrogation I should be put on trial and finally sentenced to death. On second thoughts, however, I decided that on account of my age this would probably be commuted to a life sentence which was a little disappointing for me, for whom at that time death was the finest fulfillment for the true patriot.

However, I was not there when the end finally came and the whole group, including Haridas, was arrested. We came to know that Haridas was being kept in an underground cell at the headquarters of the Intelligence Branch at Lord Sinha Road. Here he was subjected to continuous interrogation which did not allow him to sleep for days on end. With the help of a man who took food to his cell we were able to keep in touch with him and message were frequently sent and received, although he was being kept under strictest guard. Thus it was that we came to know that there was to be a secret trial. My sister, Bela, the wife of Haridas, made arrangements with a British barrister to defend her husband and a note was sent to the judge of the Special Court to give him this information. A clerk, by whom the note was sent, little knowing the legal contents of the message marched so unhesitatingly into prohibited court premises that no one made a move to prevent him. Only when the note had been delivered directly to the Judge was he seized and questioned. His innocence was so apparent however that he was allowed to go and he returned to us terrified out of his wits by this unsought escapade.

Then followed a period of great anxiety and uncertainty. Rumours flew hither and thither like wild birds. Then the final blow struck. The trial was over; sentence of death had been passed on everyone. The whole house was covered in a pall of gloom and suspense. When would the sentence be carried out? We could do nothing but wait and see.

I remember a visitor arriving one morning with the news that the end would be that very night. The members of the family were all in the last stages of despair. I was once again in the grip of an impotent rage, thinking that we sought freedom but were given death instead. Then another message came contradicting the first. My sister left for Poona to see Gandhi himself who had been released on 6th May 1944. In 1945, Lord Wavell, the then Viceroy of India who was producing the "Wavell Plan" in order to bring about greater co-operation between all political parties in the war effort against Japan, was keen to arrive at an understanding with Gandhi and Congress. In response to Gandhi's appeal on their behalf the death sentence on Haridas was commuted; the INA group were consequently committed to life imprisonment, and we were all able to breathe again.

During this period our fears were aroused on behalf of another member of the family, Sisir, who had earlier played a major part in Bose's escape to Afghanistan. He was also arrested for his role in assisting another INA group working in Calcutta. He was taken to Lahore fort, and kept prisoner there until 1946.

But to return to the war. The retreat from Imphal was only the beginning of a major evacuation of Burmah by the INA and Japanese forces. In May 1945 Rangoon fell to the British and it became apparent after the surrender of Germany that the defeat of Japan was only a matter of time. Bose, with the straggling remnants of the INA eventually reached Bangkok from where he broadcast "We may not travel to Delhi via Imphal but we shall get there alright." He was of the opinion that the more the British Indian army came to know about the INA and its heroic exploits, the stronger their sympathy would be towards it, and the more deeply they penetrated into East Asia, where the INA supporters were to be found, the more they would be convinced that "member of Azad Hind Fauz are honest patriots and revolutionaries fighting for the freedom of their motherland." They would be able to see for themselves that INA was not a puppet organization as British and Communist propaganda made it out to be. This would inspire the British Indian army to adopt an anti-British position and consequently what seemed to be a defeat would eventually prove to be a blessing in disguise. Later events amply prove this prediction to have been a valid one.

Then suddenly the war which seemed as though it might drag on for at least two years, ended with the atomic attacks on Hiroshima and Nagasaki and the surrender of Japan on 15th August 1945.

Now came the second blow. It was reported that on August 18 the aircraft carrying Bose had crashed in Formosa and that he had died of his injuries. Those was believed were filled with deep personal grief, but many remembering reports of a previous disaster were sceptical; many remain sceptical to this day. But it is certain that whether or not the report was true, with his disappearance the most inspiring chapter in India's struggle for freedom came to an end.

The three watchwords of the Azad Hind movement were unity, faith and sacrifice and these ideals were lived with amazing dedication. Never before had there been such unity between different communities, Hindus, Muslims, Sikhs, Christians and Anglo-Indians for the common cause. The immense sacrifice both of soldiers and civilians, rich and poor, men and women will constitute one of the brightest chapters in the annals of Indian history. In spite of meagre resources, and against heavy odds and in the darkest days that followed the defeat, they manifested an unconquerable faith in the destiny of India.

When Bose's activities became known after the war in India, P. Sitaramayya, the right wing candidate who contested Bose in the Congress Presidential election in 1939, wrote about him in the official history of the Congress Party :

"Suffice it for the contemporary world to know that here was a man, and every inch a 'man' that did not shine by reflected glory, that had his own inner radiance that could dare and act, for he knew the truth of the great dictum, that success often comes to those who dare and act."

The period of four and half years—from January 1941 to August 1945—when Bose tried to organise the armed struggle against British imperialism from one end of the earth to the other, Sitaramayya called "an era of miracles."

CHAPTER VI

"Bliss was in that dawn to be alive,
But to be young was very heavenly !" — Wordsworth.

The release of Mahatma Gandhi from prison in May 1944 triggered off widespread speculation concerning the possible initiative that might be taken by the British government to arrive at an understanding with the Indian National Congress. Such speculation was proved to be quite wrong, as later events showed. This action by the British government had given the impression that it no longer considered Gandhi a danger. In addition, it felt itself in a much stronger position militarily now that the USA was providing ever increasing support, and by May 1944 the INA and the Japanese forces were in full scale retreat.

It is true that President Roosevelt had unsuccessfully exerted considerable pressure upon Churchill to come to an understanding with the Indian leaders on the basis of Indian independence. The President's representative in New Delhi was consequently regarded with much suspicion and was eventually branded as a *persona non grata*. Louis Fischer, the renowned American journalist, helped considerably in putting across the Indian nationalist viewpoint to the American people and Churchill's inflexible attitude was severely criticised in the American Senate and the House of Representatives.

With the end of the war in Europe in May 1945, however, an entirely new situation developed. The Americans had paid a heavy price for the defeat of Germany and it looked as though it would take, in normal circumstances, another two years to defeat Japan. To hasten this process the USA urged the USSR to declare war against Japan and wanted India's full participation in the war, with its enormous resources of manpower. Fresh American pressure was exerted on Churchill to revive negotiations with the Indian ledaers. With the cessation of hostilities in Europe a new atmosphere of confidence had been created in Great Britain.

Lord Wavell, the then Viceroy, visited London in May 1945 and it was decided there to have a Round Table Conference on the 20th June. On the 14th June, Mr. L. S. Amery, the Secretary of State for India, said in a statement to the House of Commons that he was asking the representatives of the Congress and the Muslim League to form a government.

On the 15th June the top leaders of the Congress Party were released from prison. Six days later the Congress Working Committee met in Bombay and authorized Maulana Abul Kalam Azad, the Congress President, to represent the Party at the Round Table Conference at Simla. The Wavell Plan offered no major constitutional changes during the period of war, but the Viceroy's Executive Council would be Indianized and the Viceroy would try to create the convention that he would always act on the advice of the Council. It was the desire of the Viceroy that both the Congress Party and the Muslim League should participate in the government.

The offer was not substantially different from that of the Cripps' proposal which had been firmly rejected by the Congress three years ago. In normal circumstances there could have been no question of its being considered. But the Congress leaders, as a result of the failure of the "Quit India" movement and the success of Britain in the war, developed such a defeatist mentality that they were prepared to accept anything. This was later admitted by Maulana Azad in his book "India Wins Freedom". He said : "Once the war was over the British would have had no special reason to seek our co-operation. It was therefore not desireable for us to reject Lord Wavell's offer."

Gandhi, who had previously had been unable to reconcile himself to Indian participation in the war, was now prepared to forego his principles and he raised no objection to the Congress Party helping the war effort. The Congress Working Committee had of course formulated a face-saving formula to support its *volte face*. The differences between the British government and the Congress Party were now less since the latter was now on bended knee before its rulers.

Difficulties arose however because the leader of the Muslim League, Mohammed Ali Jinnah demanded that the Congress Party should nominate all the Hindu Members of the Council but that the Muslim members should be the nominees of the League. The Congress Party refused to be branded a Hindu party and insisted that it had the right to nominate Muslims as well. Thus the communal issue came to the forefront and fundemental political issues faded into the background. Congress was nicely caught in the trap laid for it by the British government, and eventually had to accept the partition of the country on a communal basis.

During the Simla Conference Subhas Bose made fervent appeal over the radio from the Far East to the Congress leaders to reject the Wavell Plan. He pointed out that although Britain might win the war, it would be reduced at the end of it to a second or third rate power. It would therefore be a major mistake to overestimate her strength and to underestimate the strength of the Indian people. The struggle, he said, must continue; there should be no question either of compromise or of surrender.

The second point he made was of great importance. If compromise were to be the foundation of negotiations with the British government, it would be impossible not to come to terms with all those forces which had been the main props of British rule in India, namely, the feudal lords, the communal forces, vested interests, etc. In the attempt to make all these necessary adjustments, not only would India be balkanized but many obstacles to the rapid economic and social transformation of the country would be created. But his appeal was ignored by the Congress leaders.

"Divide and rule" is the classic principle of imperialist rulers everywhere and quite understandably the British government pursued the same policy in India. No objective observer of British Indian history can deny that the British government tried to create as many divisions as possible among the Indian people so that any real advance towards independence would be thwarted by inter-communal strife. It began with the formation of the Muslim League and the introduction of a separate electorate for the Muslims. There is no doubt that the Muslims had some genuine grievances against the Hindus and therefore, it was not surprising that the British government was able to take advantage of the situation.

The British idea of promoting divisive forces was not only to postpone the day of independence as long as possible, but to divide, balkanize and weaken the conutry, when ultimately independence could no longer be withheld. In this way it could continue to maintain its influence in these parts of the country which would be carved out of the main body of India.

The strength of the Muslim League has been tested in the 1936 elections when it scored success only in some parts of the country, such as in Bengal, but it failed miserably in those areas of India which today constitute West Pakistan. It is true that during the war period while the Congress Party was banned and its leaders were under arrest, the Muslim League had full scope for extending its power and influence, But in June 1945, when it claimed at the Simla Conference the right to represent the whole Muslim population of India its strength had not been tested. Jinnah would not have dared to claim parity with the Congress Party and also the sole right to represent the Muslims, without active encouragement of at least a section of the British ruling circles.

After spending long years in prison, the Congress leaders exhibited extraordinary poverty of thinking and action when they came out. The lust for power played no small part in their make-up. Jinnah, waiting in the wings, appeared on the scene at the right moment and exploited these weaknesses of the Congress leaders to his own advantage and overnight became the key figure in the politics of compromise and parochialism. After the Simla conference the only political task left for the Congress Party was to prove that it was not entirely a Hindu organization.

It should be remembered that for the Simla conference only the rightwing leaders of the Congress were released, while all the leftist leaders and workers still remained behind prison bars. The reason for this was clear : they were opposed to any compromise with the British imperialism. Moreover, while recognising the disadvantages suffered by minorities they believed that the problem could never be solved in a piecemeal manner. Indian society comprised many religions, languages, castes and sub-castes and the ever increasing claims and counter-claims made by these groups could only lead to complete anarchy and disintegration. The unity of India had to be preserved and all sections of the people, especially the minorities, had to be assured of equality and justice.

Both these ideas were inimical to the ideas held by the British government and therefore, negotiations were conducted in their absence. Even then that failed because of the adamant attitude of the Muslim League. After this Congress leaders had no useful role to play in the political field.

In August 1945, the British Labour Party was voted into power with an overwhelming majority. The deadweight of the inflexible attitude of Churchill on the Indian question was at last lifted from the Labour Party. It was now able to formulate its policies a little more independently, although there was always the question of carrying the electorate with it and not being outmanoeuvred by the Tory opposition.

In the meantime in the middle of August, the war with Japan ended abruptly. It was announced by the British government that the general elections would be held in India in the winter of 1945-46. The Working Committee and the All India Congress Committee met in September 1945, and Gandhi expressed his opinion that there was not much hope for the Congress politically and suggested that the Congress Party should devote its time exclusively to constructive social work. However, other Congress leaders thought that the Labour government should be given a chance to prove its *bona fides* and that the Congress Party should participate in the elections. The only political issue that the Congress Party could think of was that of political amnesty. But the Viceroy, although he had ordered the release of large numbers of political prisoners, kept most of the leftist leaders, including Jayaprakash Narayan, in prison.

Without much enthusiasm the Congress issued an election manifesto and started preparing for the elections. In the many ups and downs in the history of the Congress Party this was one of the lowest points that it ever reached, both politically and morally. After its humiliation at the Simla conference there seemed nothing to look forward to but further negotiation and compromise, and the possibility of snatching at the crumbs from under the British government's table.

But within a few swift weeks the gloom and despair which pervaded the political scene in India gave way to an electrifying atmosphere of hope and elation. The magic of the INA and its leader, Netaji Subhas Chandra Bose was beginning to work.

From early October a slow trickle of released and disbanded INA soldiers, belonging to all parts of the country and every religion, began coming into contact with the Indian people. They were completely different type of Indians—men possessed by the vision of a free and united India, where every Indian was equal. They not only had the vision but had actually lived that kind of life and had fought a deathly battle for it. Although they had been defeated, they were ready to fight again and their slogan was "Jai Hind!" (Victory to India). There was none of the narrowness, apathy and despair, which prevailed all around us. At first, all this seemed incredible but slowly the idea caught on. Yes, we can be united and one; we have within us the power to overcome the might of the British empire. That we would overcome and triumph, there was no shadow of a doubt. The delirious infection of the INA started to spread swiftly through the body politic of India.

At the same time the British government in India made a major blunder in policy. It had won the war and had begun to feel that might must have been right.

The hard core of the INA consisted of the officers and men who once belonged to the British Indian army and had sworn allegiance to the British crown. Later they went over to the enemy and eventually fought against the King Emperor. They must be taught a good lesson. Moreoveаr, the British government felt that the loyal British Indian army officers and men should be shown what fate awaited them if they rebelled against British power in the future. This would have been the natural approach for a victor country in a normal situation, but at the end of 1945 the situation in India could hardly be called normal. Although there was an apparent lull in the political situation and the defeatist mentality manifested by the Congress leaders con vinced the rulers that the British government was invincible, they completely underestimated the tremendously explosive and inflammable nature of the INA and Subhas Bose, which was about to upset all normal calculations.

The second blunder, which also emanated from overconfidence was that the trial of INA officers was to be open so as to make public the "treacherous" activities of these officers. Each day's proceedings in the Court came out in the next day's newspapers and every small detail of the INA activities spread swiftly throughout the country. The trial was followed by the people with mounting excitement, caused not by the treachery of these persons but by their burning patriotism and spirit of sacrifice. In fact, the open trial had just the opposite effect to that which the British government had expected. Instead of frightening a demoralised people, it aroused a sleeping nation.

The third mistake was, that for the first trial, the government had chosen three officers, Shah Nawaz Khan, Prem Sehgal and Gurubaksh Singh Dhillon, who belonged to Muslim, Hindu and Sikh communities respectively. For the Indian people they symbolised the unity of the religious communities in the INA and their willingness to fight shoulder to shoulder in a common cause.

On the 21st November 1945, the first trial of the INA officers started at the Red Fort in Delhi. It was the signal for the beginning of the post-war revolution in India, which culminated in the revolt of the Royal Indian Navy in February 1946. These three months of widespread revolt of all sections of the Indian people proved beyond any shadow of doubt that it would no longer be possible for the British government to cling on to power in India. It had lost control of the British Indian Army, Navy, Airforce and Police through which it exercised its power. Moreover, the INA traitors had become for most of the British Indian forces either "heroes" or a continued source of pangs in their conscience.

The spark of the post-war revolution was ignited by the students of Calcutta when on the 21st November they came out of their classes and in a massive demonstration marched towards the Government House to demand the release of the INA officers. They were stopped at the outer limits of the prohibited area where the Government House and the Secretariat were situated. They broke the cordon and the police opened fire. One student, Rameshwar Bannerjee, was killed and several others were seriously injured.

When I heard about it, I rushed to the spot. It was a very difficult place to reach as a vast area was cordoned off by the police so that others could not join the students who were squatting in Dharamtolla Street. All the shops and offices were closed, the traffic was diverted and the area was filled with tension and the expectancy of new struggles and deaths. After many detours and stratagems I reached the place where the excited students, held back by the police, were shouting slogans. I promptly squatted on the street and joined in. I soon gathered that there were differences about the course of action to be adopted; one set of student leaders were for breaking the cordon once again and facing the consequences; others said that they should seek the guidance of political leaders before they took the next step. Although I was in favour of breaking the cordon, I decided to abide by whatever decision was taken by the majority.

Several second and third rank political leaders came and addressed the gathering. Most of them, while supporting the students, cautioned them against rash action. The students were getting restive and were unable to make up their minds, but those who were advocating taking impotent revenge on the killers of their comrades, were getting the maximum response.

The students called for the guidance of Sarat Chandra Bose, the elder brother of Subhas Bose, who had been released sometime previously from prison. An outstanding lawyer, besides generously supporting Subhas Bose financially, he was connected mainly with the Legislative wing of the Congress Party and was also a member of the Congress Working Committee. In the absence of Subhas Bose from the political scene, many people expected, wrongly as later events proved, that he would provide the leadership in this revolutionary situation. We waited in vain for him, but he never came. We were bitterly disappointed. Without his guidance, it was eventually decided that we would not leave but stay on where we were for the whole night. We expected that the news would spread and the next day the students and others would join and a new decision would be taken on the basis of newly acquired strength.

I decided to stay on because as it became late, the crowd started thinning out and it would have been terrible if everybody had gone home in spite of the decision to stay. Going away would have seemed like desertion. I had come without telling my family who, I knew, must be worried about my absence, but there was no way of informing them where I was. The late November night began to get cold and I shivered in my thin clothes.

At one stage the Governor of Bengal, Sir Richard Casey,

who later became the External Affairs Minister and the Governor-General of Australia, came on the other side of the police cordon in his immaculate dress suit and tried to address the students over the microphone standing on a police van. But we greeted him with shouts of "Go back Casey, the murderer!" After several attempts to speak, he left disappointed.

All the money we had we gave away so that some hot tea and biscuits could be bought and distributed among the students. I felt a deep sense of affinity and comradeship with all these people who were unknown to each other a few hours ago.

Time passed on slowly. We overcame our drowsiness by occasional bursts of slogan shouting. When it was quiet we thought and talked about what the morrow would bring. Especially for those who were in favour of breaking the cordon, of whom I was one, we knew many of us might not be alive the next day. Somehow it seemed that it did not matter for us ourselves but it did matter a lot for the freedom struggle. On this night and the following days I realised the psychological make-up of a revolutionary upsurge and what it meant for individuals and the mass in which they are lost.

The next three months was the most satisfying and hopeful time for India I have lived through. After the immediately preceding period of despair and hopelessness, slowly confidence, pride and hope emerged in us and in no time the pace of events increased and became a surging flood capable of sweeping aside all before it. There were many things which needed to be smashed besides British imperialism but we felt not only hatred and the desire for destruction; we wanted to build a new and free India — a society free of exploitation and greed and based on the brotherhood of man.

We were torn out of our small personal lives. Leaving our homes we rushed out in the streets, got mixed up with everybody else and were lost in the crowd. What a terrific power it possessed! We created the monster demonstrations which had one purpose common to us all — the freedom of our country. It was a peculiar twilight region between individuality and collectivity — "one for all, and all for one". That cold night of 21st November I became a denizen of that twilight world. I, a drop of rain, acquired the strength of a flood and its irresistible surge.

It was a unique, exhilirating feeling — being on the crest of a revolutionary wave.

It was the stuff of which history is made. After its sweep nothing could remain the same any more. For us, it meant the destruction of British imperialism and the advent of a new dawn in which we would create a heaven on earth. To be young in such a time and to be able to act, to give one's life away, if necessary, was simply heavenly!

We were no more afraid. In the fight we might be injured and suffer pain but it would be something more than an individual pain. In the battle we might die : that would be the end of the self but not for the people. We acquired another dimension in our existence which transformed the basic quality of our lives. It was like a new birth. Through this new birth, the birth of a new nation slowly took shape. One could feel all the agonies and ecstacies of this difficult birth in those shining and unforgettable days.

We were keenly waiting for the sun to rise. It was still dark when the first newspapers came whose headlines flared with the incidents of the day before. Seeing the photographs and the news that the students had maintained the whole night vigil, we had no doubt that thousands of people would come to the spot within a few hours and swell the ranks and the second round of the battle would begin.

A few generous sympathisers made some contributions and we managed to have a cup of tea. By 9 a.m. the demonstrators had increased to thousands and the crowd was swaying and bursting. It was decided not to break the cordon but to march to the northern part of the city and to carry the dead body of Rameshwar Bannerjee to cremation ground in the south. As the procession proceeded it grew and grew until it became one of the biggest demonstrations that Calcutta had ever witnessed. People in thousands lined the streets, showering flowers and responding to the slogans with great gusto. It was hard to believe that within twenty four hours the whole atmosphere in Calcutta could be so radically changed.

It was one of the longest marches I had undertaken on an empty stomach. The whole day this mass of humanity wound through the streets of Calcutta igniting the fires of rebellion. Nobody could have dreamed that there could be such a magnificent response from the people. The struggle had started and was soon to spread to every corner of the country. The bell started to toll for British imperialism.

When I returned home twenty four hours later, thoroughly exhausted, I was soundly rebuked. Why I had not said where I was going? They had spent hours enquiring in police stations and hospitals. I did not answer and went silently to bed. Nothing could detract from the feeling of satisfaction that I had been one of those who had helped in turning the protest started by a few hundred of students into a massive demonstrations involving hundreds of thousands.

The following days and weeks were full of demonstrations, public meetings, discussions, strikes, arrests, lathi-charges, tear gas, firing and charges by the mounted police. The whole country was afire! The struggle started by the students had spread to the workers, peasants, teachers and eventually to the police and the armed forces. The most spectacular and decisive action was the mutiny of the Royal Indian Navy. Starting with grievances of ratings it ended with the full-fledged fight for independence. The British government by this time was so desperate that it was prepared to destroy the whole Navy in order to quell the revolt.

The tremendous mass upsurge not only frightened the British government but also unnerved the leaders of the Congress Party and the Muslim League. Subhas Bose and the INA provided the main inspiration and the revolutionary upsurge was throwing up new leadership. If the events were allowed to continue in this way then not only the British government but also the leadership of the Congress and Muslim League would be swept aside. It seemed all the three had vested interest in arresting the revolutionary wave from spreading. Sardar Vallabbhai Patel, the leader of Congress rightwing, made the utmost efforts to bring the naval ratings in Bombay "to their senses" and eventually the mutiny was quelled.

But the mighty struggle of three months had by then clinched the issue of the British rule in India. It was impossible to keep India in bondage anymore. On March 15, 1946, the British Prime Minister, Clement Attlee made a statement in the House of Commons in which he frankly admitted the the conception of nationalism in India had continued to grow stronger and had now permeated even the armed forces. The situation, he said, had completely changed and demanded a new approach. He announced that a Cabinet Mission would go to India to resolve the problem.

Indian Nationalism had scored a decisive victory in the first round of the battle, but alas, the victory was to be shortlived.

CHAPTER VII

> "The great events with which old story ring
> Seem vain and hollow; I find nothing great,
> Nothing is left that I can venerate." — Wordsworth.

The tragic and tangled history of India from the 15th March 1946, when Attlee made his announcement regarding the arrival of the Cabinet Mission, to the 14th-15th August, 1947, when power was transferred to the Dominions of Pakistan and Indian Union has been written in the minutest detail by innumerable Indian and British authors. There seems to be no point, therefore, in repeating it here. Moreover, from a personal point of view I would feel no pleasure in remembering and recounting a painful story, which I only want to forget.

How I wish that these sixteen crucial blood-stained months and all the evil consequences they left behind could be obliterated from the pages of Indian history. But that cannot be done. In fact, most of the acute problems that we have been facing for the last two decades had been the consequences of these very events. They have to be faced squarely and accepted. Then only can we dare to overcome them. The evasion of facts and truths can never be a guide to the solution of problems — either individual or national.

During this period all that is worst in Indian life came out and manifested itself fully. The atmosphere was filled with the most virulent forms of pettiness, rabid communalist fanaticism and unspeakable savagery. The political scene was dominated by tired, power-hungry and small men who, with their combined efforts, managed to unleash the biggest civilian holocaust in the annals of twentieth century. Gandhi, the only person with a touch of greatness, became increasingly ineffective and slowly faded out. He tried to undo the evil effects of communal passion in his own individual style with only partial success. After independence an assasin's bullet saved him from being reduced to a "nuisance" and embarrassment to the new Indian government.

Only five months separated Attlee's announcement about the

Cabinet Mission and the beginning of the "Great Calcutta Killing" of Hindus and Muslims on the 16th August, 1946. Within this short time the combined efforts of the British government, the Congress Party and the Muslim League managed to transform the fullscale popular national upheaval into squalid, nauseating Hindu-Muslim rioting. The zig zag course of the high level negotiations in New Delhi resulted in two things. The people at large had no other role to play except to read newspapers and to talk about the problems. Secondly, all other issues faded into the background and the communal issue came to the forefront, with the Muslim League taking an increasingly aggressive attitude. The Cabinet Mission made a proposal about the future set-up of India with a federal structure, the Central Government having only Defence, Foreign Affairs and Communications. The country was to be divided into three groups, one constituting the Hindu majority area and the other two constituting the Muslim majority areas in north western and north eastern areas of India. In spite of the leftist opposition, the Congress Party accepted the proposal. The Muslim League also accepted it. However, at a later stage certain remarks of the newly elected Congress President, Jawaharlal Nehru about the Cabinet Mission Plan made the Muslim League retract its position and demanded the establishment of a separate independent State of Pakistan. It further decided to launch the "Direct Action Day" on the 16th August to back up their demand. This proved to be the turning point of the tragic history of India.

At that time a Muslim League Ministry under the Chief Ministership of H. S. Suhrwardy was ruling Bengal. The government declared the 16th August a public holiday throughout Bengal so that the day could be observed in a befitting manner. The Muslim League had coined the provocative slogan : *Larke Lenge Pakistan,* meaning "We will achieve Pakistan by fighting". Tension had in the meantime built up. There was widespread apprehension that there could be an eruption of communal rioting on an extensive scale.

By that time I was, along with my friend Francis Subhas Biswas, one of the organizers of the Azad Hind Dal, a paramilitary volunteer organization based on the ideals of the INA. We decided to have a route march through the streets of Calcutta with white flags, appealing to the people to maintain communal harmony and peace. Starting early in the morning of the fateful day of 16th August, we marched through both Hindu and Muslim localities for nearly five hours. The streets were mostly deserted with no vehicular traffic as it was not only a holiday but also an imposed general strike. No untoward incident took place while we were marching. We ended our march at noon and within two hours the cruellest and the most widespread riot of the contemporary history of Calcutta broke out.

As soon as we heard the reports that a nearby market place was being looted, some of the volunteers were immediately rushed to the spot armed with *lathis* (long thick bamboo sticks). We were ordered to beat up the looters, to stop the looting and to protect the shops, as the police were nowhere in sight. This was a Hindu area and therefore, the Muslim shops were the targets. Within a short time, we cleared the shops of the looters and posted volunteers in front of each of the shops. But the volunteers were few and the crowd was immense. Slowly the demagogues started to incite the mob against the volunteers, who were mostly Hindus. "If you have so much courage, why don't you go and protect the Hindu shops in the Muslim areas?" They began to enumerate incidents of looting and killing by the Muslim League volunteers in different parts of the city, some of which were true, as we came to know later, and some were just wild, mischievous rumours. Soon there were heated altercations between the volunteers and the mob. "Let us kill the Muslim agents first, before we kill the Muslims", someone shouted and the mob started attacking the volunteers. One of the volunteers would have been killed on the spot unless some of the INA men had intervened and saved him. The INA men requested the volunteers to withdraw because it would be impossible to stop such mob fury with *lathis.* The volunteers were withdrawn and the looting was resumed.

Here we were experiencing another upsurge of popular emotion but this time there was no feeling of unity only a narrow, negative communal passion with its blind and savage strength. One felt helpless in the face of it, because we had ceased to speak a commonly understood language.

On this day there was a big rally to observe the Direct Action Day at the *maidan,* the only wide open space in Calcutta. Huge armed Muslim League processions started coming from all direction towards the meeting place. Looting and killing by the League volunteers began to take place even before the processions arrived. The police were deliberately kept away to give free hands to the *goondas* to do whatever they liked. Innocent men, women and children were killed in hundreds. The day was supposed to be observed as a protest against the British government for not granting Pakistan but curiously the only citizens who felt safe in those days were the British.

By the evening the rioting had spread to all parts of the city. Thousands of dead bodies littered the streets of Calcutta. The houses of the Muslims in Hindu areas and of the Hindus in Muslim areas were attacked. Killing, raping, maiming and looting went on unchecked. While the storm raged, for nearly forty-eight hours there was no administration in the city. The leading English daily of Calcutta, *The Statesman,* whose British editor had pronouncedly pro-Muslim attitude, said in the editorial that there was a deliberate plan behind this fury. The full-scale struggle for Pakistan had been launched with unbelievable cynicism and cruelty and with the indirect support of the Government.

On the second day the Hindus and Sikhs began to retaliate on a big scale. Then only did the Muslim League administration call in the police and the Army to control the situation. They patrolled the main streets, while in the side streets and by-lanes killing continued. Rescue operations started and soon the schools and colleges were filled with refugees.

We, who were supposed to be freedom fighters, started rescuing one set of Indians from being killed by another set of Indians. What an anti-climax! During the daytime we were looking after the well being of the refugees in our area, while at night we guarded the locality from the possible Muslim attack. This was counter-revolution *par excellence*. After the first spate of killing in Calcutta, Jinnah and Nehru issued statements condemning violence but they were too busy to pay a visit to the afflicted humanity in Calcutta.

The only bright feature in this tragic story was the tales of how some Hindus and Muslims risked their lives to save their neighbours of the other community. There was still a spark of humanity left in the midst of man's indescribable inhumanity to man, but all our beautiful dreams were drowned in the blood of innocent men.

For one complete year intermittent killing went on in Calcutta making life in the city uncertain and risky. Then the riots spread to Noakhali in East Bengal, a predominantly Muslim area. The wild revenge for this was taken in the predominantly Hindu areas of Bihar. Gandhi was running about from Calcutta to Noakhali and Bihar desperately trying to ease communal passion, while his disciples Nehru and Patel were busy preparing to divide the country on a communal basis. Their feeling of "nationalism" had been burnt up by the raging flame of communalism. They did not have the guts to say 'no' to partition, come what may. They were tired and weak men who wanted power even if it meant sacrificing their principles.

On the 15th August 1947, power was transferred to truncated India. The Forward Bloc, to which I belonged, called it a day of mourning. It signified the defeat of Indian nationalism and the triumph of 'divide and rule' policy of the British imperialism, as it led to the partition of the country on religious basis. We marched in a silent procession through the streets of Calcutta. Then amazingly the atmosphere of Calcutta, marred for the last one year by communal rioting, completely changed. Everywhere was joy and elation. People loaded on to trucks, buses, jeeps and private cars, bedecked with national flag, were moving about freely in the streets shouting slogans with complete abandon. Our solemn march seemed completely out of tune with the spirit of the city. The same evening the unbelievable happened; Hindus began visiting the Muslim areas, which they would never have dared to do for the last one year; and the Muslims came to the Hindu areas. There were universal demonstrations of amity and peace. Calcutta is indeed a strange city with its amazing capacity of reacting, always with vigour, to different situations.

But the surgical operation on the country had been accomplished at an astronomical cost especially in the Punjab. During the nine months after independence, it is estimated that 16 million people were forced to leave their homes and became refugees in strange places. In the same period nearly 600,000 were killed and nearly 100,000 young girls were kidnapped by both sides, forcibly converted or sold on the auction.

This, in addition to what had happened earlier in Calcutta, Noakhali and Bihar, is the price we paid for our Dominion Status in a divided country. We were told by Congress propaganda that we had attained our freedom in a non-violent way and the transfer of power from Britain was "voluntary" and "peaceful". Those lies are still dished out in India and in Britain. It was a nasty piece of job for which any honourable man will have nothing but a feeling of shame. That is the heritage that has been bequeathed to us.

If there had been a straight violent struggle against Britain there would have been far less loss of life; the struggle would have bound the different sections of the Indian people together, the physical operation on the country would not have been necessary and a strong, united and free India would have emerged.

Instead, we divided the country on the patently absurd "two-nation" theory of Jinnah, which asserted that religion constitutes the basis of a nation and the people who professed Islam were a different nation and therefore, needed a homeland. The justification for division was that it would solve once and for all the Hindu-Muslim communal problem. Yes, that would have been possible if there was a complete transfer of population — Muslims to Pakistan and Hindus to India. But that did not happen and it was Jinnah who was firmly opposed to that idea. So Muslims remained in India and Hindus in East Pakistan and the problem remained with us two decades after independence. Everything seemed to have been based on myths and falsehood. One could only hope when sanity and common humanity (the two qualities which were singularly absent in those days) return all these absurdities will be fully realized.

India had obviously missed a great chance to prove its worth. Such chances come rarely in a nation's life. Not only that, a great betrayal was perpetrated by the leaders. I could not accept their leadership.

When I looked around me after the attainment of independence, I had no doubt that this was not the kind of India I wanted to die for.

What kind of India I did want to die for and how it could be attained, I did not have any clear picture; nor was I aware of the complexities which the answer to that question involved.

I made up my mind that I must know the answer. Profoundly disillusioned I withdrew from politics and decided to spend at least ten years finding out the answers to my innumerable questions.

I had a vision of a free India which was completely distorted by the reality. Is that an inevitable process? Cannot there be a vision which is realistic enough to be transformed into reality? I did not know, but I wanted to find that out.

It was not only the macrocosmic vision of India but also its microcosmic manifestations which interested me. I wanted to study the role of the individual in the transformation of the Indian society. So gradually the phase of political activities came to an end and the period of intellectual quest began.

PART TWO

PERSONAL EXPLORATIONS

CHAPTER I

"Love is not merely looking at each other but also towards the same direction."—Saint-Exupery.

I had already developed a deep interest in the freedom struggle when I felt the first awakening of a whole new range of feelings and emotions which disturbed and troubled me; life seemed to assume a new dimension where the pulse beat faster, and moods moved from ecstasy to the deepest melancholy; where dreams and reality became inextricably confused and where the self seemed shattered, like moonlight on water when wind blows and one longed for the moment when the breeze would be stilled and the reflection be once more whole and complete.

I became acutely conscious of my body and its physical needs but the dominating purpose of my life was still to play my part in the fight for independence and I did not intend that anything should stand in the way of this overruling passion. It could not of course subjugate the urgent desires and longings which beset me but my attitude towards such feelings was marked by the determination that passion should never supersede politics!

When I was a boy the whole social pattern which governed the relationship between the sexes was much more rigid, even in the city, then it is today. Boys and girls who were not close relations were kept separate and for me to know a girl who was not a close relative was a virtual impossibility. It is true that exceptionally smart young men seemed able to break through the barrier but I unfortunately did not belong to this group! Consequently, there was no development of any kind of natural friendship with the opposite sex and the only remaining possibility was a recourse to flights of fancy into a dream world of illusion and romance.

Growing up in such an atmosphere it was inevitable that young adolescents should be overtly affected by any others in their immediate environment. The boys and girls in the neighbouring houses became the centre of one's interests. One learnt from observation the routine of their lives: at what time of the day they would appear on the verandah to become the cynosure of all eyes; the hour they would leave for school and the time of their return. How eloquent were the silent longing stares across the street! No words were ever spoken, only the mute exchange of half-embarrassed glances, like Donne's lovers.

"Our eye-beams twisted and did thread
Our eyes, upon one double-string."

I remember the different kinds of reaction which such observations evoked on the part of the girls. Most, overcome by shyness, would withdraw almost immediately; others would take refuge in exaggerated action, talk loudly to someone, begin a game of exceptional gusto with children or display a sudden interest in the household work to attract attention; still others would assume an expression of infinite sadness as though conscious of the tragedy of separation, of being so near and yet so far away. I was no exception in suffering from this common malady of "neighbourly love". And this in spite of myself, for I had the conviction that love was a trap leading to the bondage of marriage and I wanted to remain aloof from it all and free to serve my country with single-minded devotion. Love could not be divided; women and gold, I thought tempt men not only away from God but also from the path of true patriotism!

For a boy, the temptation of gold is not one likely to move him so much, but girls! Ah! that was a different matter. Somehow one could not help being attracted to them, for all the attendant risks and dangers. But they seemed remote creatures walking lightly over the surface of the world like goddesses, unconscious of we, poor male mortals, who would willingly have thrown ourselves at their feet. To win the heart of one such of these must be one of the most difficult things in life, I thought. I knew this from my elder sisters and cousins. If I accompanied them for walks in the parks or by the riverside I noticed how other boys would show interest in them and perhaps would even follow them at a distance. But all they got for their trouble were contemptuous remarks from the solid safety of the female group, and the boys, I sadly noted, had no chance at all.

Yet how trivial an incident it was which transformed my pessimism into a qualified optimism. I was, I suppose, fifteen or sixteen at the time and had secretly and sorrowfully lost my heart to the girl next door. I had heard that she was very intelligent and from her behaviour she was clearly a bright and lively person. When I passed her house my eyes were irresistibly drawn towards the windows to try to catch a glimpse of the laughing eyes, the dark shining hair, or best of all to find her silently leaning over the balcony to exchange a long wistful look before I hurried down the road. Yet I had visited their house often. There was a lawn where I frequently went to play cricket or badminton with the boys in the family. But though the girls would sometimes watch our games from the upper rooms we never spoke; our worlds never met except in the realm of the imagination.

Then one day my cousin sister who lived with us and attended the same school as A. came in great excitement.

"I was with A. when you passed by," she exclained, "and she confessed to me that she liked you."

I stared at her in utter disbelief. Then I was caught up in the most delightful confusion. Could the news really be true? But I had nothing that could make her like or admire me; I had never spoken a single word or written one line to express my feelings for her. On the other hand, her rather self-conscious gaiety in my presence did, I thought, indicate that perhaps she had some interest in me. Then if that were true it must mean that I had some qualities that a girl might like. This seemed scarcely credible. Yet there was no way in which I could discover whether or not it were true. As the days went by she became an obsession for me. If I did not see her, the whole of life seemed empty and meaningless; when she was there I felt an uncontrollable longing to come closer, which was impossible.

Then I left Calcutta and went to stay for a time with my brother, Kalyan in Jamshedpur. But separation in space made no difference. I could not apply my mind to anything. I felt suffocated by the impossibility of giving vent to my feelings and at last in a mood of desperation I came to a daring decision. I wrote her a short letter asking whether she would agree to having a penfriendship with me. Having completed it I could hardly believe in my own audacity. I could not post it of course. I put the letter in my pocket and went out. I came to a post box and stopped. I felt sick. The letter was lying there where I had put it. I ran my fingers over the envelope, smooth and harmless. I had only to drop it and perhaps the whole of my life would be changed; but I could not do it. I walked on. I must have passed a dozen boxes and at each one went through the same agony of suspense. At last I came to the main post office and in a sudden blind moment of action I shoved the letter into the box. It was done! Irrevocably. Now there was nothing for it but to wait to see what would be the consequences of my indiscretion. During the following week, long before the postal delivery time I would wait on the verandah for the postman's footstep. Many letters came during the ensuing days but the one I longed for, never.

When I returned to Calcutta with heavy heart I thought that having already taken so unconventional a step, I should already have lost any prestige I ever had, so I sent another note to her through a servant enquiring whether she had received the one sent from Jamshedpur. Again there was no answer and to this day I do not know whether either of them ever reached her. Perhaps they were intercepted by the elders; perhaps she read them but was ordered not to reply, or perhaps she simply did not want to encourage me. In defence of my self-esteem I arrived at the happy conclusion that although she could like and admire me from a distance, circumstances made it impossible for her to communicate her liking.

I have always regretted that she never knew how indebted I was to her. She gave me a store of self-confidence by making me believe that I was a person of some worth. Whether or not her admiration was real or fictional was never really proved but it was real enough for me to think that perhaps winning the hearts of those exotic creatures was not such an insuperable task after all.

Now although this introduction into the unexplored realm of boy-girl relationships did not bring me any sense of completeness or fulfillment, it kindled in my imagination ideas about developing a mature and balanced expression of affection and friendship. This only accentuated my loneliness and urged me on to find some one with whom such a bond could be forged. Friendship with a boy would not suffice. I wanted the doubled intensity that friendship with a girl could provide, but it was quite definitely 'friendship' on which I had set my heart, "nothing more, nothing less." Something more would have meant "love", and love, I thought, led to marriage and marriage was out, as far as I was concerned. Yet anything less than real friendship was not worthwhile. I asked myself "What did I mean by this friendship?" And it seemed that primarily I wanted to find someone with whom I could establish communication, that is, the sense of freedom which comes from frank and open expression of thoughts, emotions and ideas, an expression which spontaneously evokes a warm and understanding response. Along with this, I wanted both of us to be inspired by common ideals and interests (which at that time meant that my hypothetical friend must have whole-hearted enthusiasm for the freedom struggle); but although I expected that warm feelings, perhaps even bordering on love might exist, I wanted the relationship to be maintained without sex coming into it at all. My "revolutionary" attitude were, it seemed, confined to politics! When it came to matters of the heart I remained the most rigid conventionalist. Sex, outside the framework of marriage, if not exactly a sin for which one could be damned eternally, was, to say the least, a lamentable failure of character, only to be committed by the weak. I did not want to consider myself weak and consequently clung steadfastly to the codes of conventional morality.

My first experiment in friendship with a girl, however, was doomed to failure. The girl was a classmate in the co-educational college which I attended. To get to know any of the girls personally was in itself a major problem. They used to enter the class as a group after the professor and retreat, before he left, into the safety of the ladies' common room and it required real perseverance and ingenuity to overcome this segregation.

From my vantage point on the back row I was able to obtain a good view of the other students without myself being observed and I was immediately drawn to B who seemed of all the girls in the class not only one of the most attractive but certainly the most intelligent. It took all my courage and much subtle engineering before I could get myself introduced but I eventually succeeded and after a few casual exchanges I wrote her a letter suggesting that we might be friends. I later learnt that this was only one of many letters which she received from numerous admirers, but apparently she found a directness in mine which appealed to her and she showed it to her mother and sister for their approval. This was evidently favourable as I soon received an answer to say that she was agreeable.

After this we met frequently outside the college. Everything went as I had hoped. We talked and talked endlessly. When we were apart we wrote long letters containing our discussions. We understood one another very well; we had ideals in common and the whole relationship seemed to me to be progressing in exactly the way I had planned. I was full of affection for her and delighted in her company and sex was never a disturbing factor. So we continued in this cool, delightful fashion until almost a year had passed by.

Then one day I was brought down from the clouds in no uncertain manner. A letter arrived from her (no unusual event) but its contents were far from being the usual friendly exchange of ideas. Through skillfully contrived phrases in which nothing was stated directly, she nevertheless managed to convey quite clearly that she was in love with me, that she wanted to marry me, and that if this did not happen her life would no longer be worth living.

This letter began a period of intense argument and conflict. Obviously I had been mistaken in thinking that my ideas of true friendship were being worked out in practice. She had not shared my ideals at all and merely tolerated them, for the sake of the kind of relationship which she had in mind. Really we had both been working towards entirely different ends. The only possible solution now was to bring the whole affair to a friendly but definite conclusion so that she could divert her attention to some one more satisfactory, but she would not agree. Henceforward, she insisted, she would offer the kind of friendship I sought. So it dragged on for a time, I realising the futility of the situation, she hoping that I would change my mind and disharmony jarred the atmosphere of our infrequent meetings.

She was to leave Calcutta on a holiday. We decided to meet before her departure and we went for tea to Ferazzini's. She looked different. She was wearing a blouse of very thin, transparent material and had made herself up carefully. She was her brightest and gayest self and it seemed as though something of the former warmth returned between us. When we came out it was almost dark.

"What do you want to do now?" I asked.

"I am not in a great hurry. Let's go for a walk."

"Which way "

"This way," and she led across Chowringhee towards the maidan.

I allowed myself to be led. We walked along the road towards the river in cool December evening, the moonlight drenching the fields with silver.

After a while she said : "Let's sit down." The grass was soaked with dew.

"We can't sit here, you will get your fine clothes wet."

"Who cares about clothes ?" she flung herself down on the ground. I carefully calculated the distance and seated myself about six feet away, but almost immediately she dived into her handbag and fetching out an autograph album announced that I must write something in it. She came over to where I was and sat down beside me to see what I would write. I thought for a while and then wrote some words of Longfellow :

"Lives of all great men remind us that we can make our lives sublime." I added : "Is it just a saying or something more ? I would like you to answer this question with your life."

As my pen moved over the velvety surface of the paper she learned across to see what I would write. I knew as her cheek came closer to mine, that I was nearing the edge of the precipice and that unless I was to pitch forward into the unknown darkness, now was the time to beat a hasty retreat. But I did not want to hurt her feelings or make her think that she had been indiscreet. I waited a while trying to make myself sound casual and unconcerned in a few general observations.

Then "I shall have to go now. I have some work I must do."

"You did not say you had to work before."

I was silent.

"Well, I do not want to go," she said, "please stay on."

"Then I am sorry," I tried to speak gently, "but I have to leave now" and I struggled up from the wet grass. Reluctantly she too rose and we set off towards the bus stop. My futile attempts to make conversation were met with a stubborn and angry silence.

It was sad I thought. The leap from the precipice had been for her the whole meaning and purpose of the evening.

She had wanted to add a new dimension to the relationship and she was probably right in thinking that if she could succeed in doing this then our association would have proceeded in the direction that she had hoped.

Even today when my ideas regarding sexual expression are completely changed I still think that I was right. To have behaved differently would have been to act in the grip of a momentary weakness which ran contrary to my inner convictions and in doing so I should have lost all respect not only for myself but also for the person who had urged me on.

As it happened I was even more affected by her absence after we ceased to meet. Her sadness touched me, where her anger and coquettry had left me cold. From her I learnt something of the immense complexities which make up a personality. I discovered that human relationships cannot be made to order, and my conception of "friendship" was too unrealistic. Women, I decided, were not capable of maintaining that delicate balance which was needed. They were all too ready to topple over into the realm of love.

The most important revelation however was the terrifying ease with which words could become distorted to convey an entirely different meaning from the one intended.

"If you had made your intentions clear in the beginning," she had accused me, "I should have set my sail for a different wind." My letters, she had said, had expressed love; all her friends had told her so.

"Show me. Show me where I have said it."

"Well.... not in so many words."

It was a complete failure of communication. Words written in friendship were read as words of love.

"I have realised my mistake too late to be of any help to you," I said. "But perhaps someone else will reap the benefit. Next time it shall be made crystal from the first words, what I mean by friendship, what I mean by love."

After this disaster I grew very pessimistic about the possibility of developing the relationship I had envisaged. Yet I continued to cling to my conception of friendship, although it had already proved a failure, simply because I could think of no other alternative. About this time however a change occurred in my total outlook which also affected my attitude towards women.

After India attained independence I felt thoroughly let down. This was not what I wanted to die for. The urge for self-sacrifice sank into the background and was gradually replaced by an impetus of a different kind. I wanted

"To follow knowledge like a sinking star,
Beyond the utmost bounds of human thought."

I wanted experience of all kinds. I wanted to observe and watch; I became a "spectator of all time and of all existence" and I was no longer so keen on recruiting women as freedom fighters but grew more interested in understanding them as people. I wanted to get away from Calcutta with all its ties and memories and find some place where I could enter upon a "new life." I was fortunate and managed to get a job in one of the most beautiful hill stations in South India, Kodaikanal, as a manager of a multi-purpose business enterprise, which included an agricultural farm, a photographic studio, a sports goods shop, a bakery and a restaurant. C was one of the girls who used to come to the restaurant.

She did not interest me at all. Physically she was not attractive. She was in fact rather a masculine type, short, sturdy and much devoted to energetic games. She seemed shallow and superficial and exhibited a crude kind of sex appeal with her tight jeans and shirt blouses.

One day she appeared in one of the inner rooms of the building, looking for records to relay in the restaurant. I looked up from what I was doing and studied her. "Why are you so self-conscious ?" I asked. With that question I turned the corner which was to lead me into unexplored country. I came to know the other side of the coin. She had an aesthetic sensitivity which found expression in her painting and music. A brusque exterior hid tumult, turmoil and "divine disquiet"; she possessed a mind which sent out questioning tendrils to know and understand the world about her. She had the ability to pierce the barriers which society builds around individuals, with astonishing abandon. She turned all my preconceived ideas about "charming girls" upside down. My last romantic conceptions of fragile, dainty ladies were swept away. "Charming" took on a new connotation; it implied the possession of a feminine form but a mind which could compete on equal terms with men. Unbelievably this girl, not in the least pretty, with contours that no connoisseur of female beauty would look at twice, short, snubbed-nosed, athletic, became for me the epitome of all charm, the sum of all delight.

But I was cautious. I had no intention of committing my first mistake again. I chose my words carefully and explained in great detail my theories about "friendship." Was such a thing possible? I asked her. I told her about my previous experience and its failure. She was sympathetic. The kind of relationship I had described was just what she had wanted. Her great ambition was to be an artist and to this end she wanted to devote herself, but friendship with someone of like interests would not interfere with this. I believed her. What was more she was a European and seemed to me to be capable of a more objective view than most Indian women. "But", she demanded, "why are you afraid of sex?" This pulled me up short. Was it true? Was I afraid of sex?

One thing was certain, in no time at all I was madly in love. Yet I was opposed to love and much disturbed within myself as to whether I should deliberately hold myself in check or lose myself in all the unknown delights that love held in store. Should I make a valiant effort to maintain that "delicate balance" (of which women were incapable) or give up the struggle and go whole-hoggedly after experience. I was full of doubts about the expression of friendship. Was it possible to be in love and yet not commit oneself to marriage? Why should friendship between men and women be platonic? Was physical expression wrong between two people feeling affection for one another? If such expression took place, did it mean that friendship had ended and love begun? Should love which leads to marriage be anything more than friendship plus sex? Was there no half-way house between platonic friendship and love which led to marriage?

All this time I seemed to be taking up quite a different position in relation to sex from that adopted in cultural milieu in which I was brought up. Was I rationalizing my own weakness, I wondered. I was beginning to question the efficacy of the rigid conventional moral code which I had followed until then. Why should I not express myself? What was the harm?

Because an idea had been practised unquestioningly for thousands of years, it did not seem to me that it was necessarily right. I wanted to be convinced by reason and not because it was laid down in the *shastras*.

Ultimately all my ruminations on ethics boiled down to one direct and important question : to kiss or not to kiss

C's mother's return from Europe was imminent and whether she would approve of our friendship was doubtful. We knew the end might be soon, and although we had spent hours discussing the physical expression of love, I, at twentythree years of age, had never yet attempted to put theory into practice. With my new drive for knowledge and experience this seemed to me a distinct handicap which should be overcome as soon as possible. I had convinced myself by now that there was nothing wrong in kissing. As a European C would surely have none of my inhibitions and as the day of her mother's arrival drew closer, the desire to kiss grew stronger and stronger until it occupied all my waking thoughts. To take the initiative seemed to be a tremendous problem and I was seized with a peculiar lethargy until the final day dawned. It was, I remember, a Saturday and the American school, where she was a student was closed. In the morning C came over to the restaurant. I had to act quickly. But how? I could not simply grab and kiss her.

She said that she could not stay long and so I had little time for pondering. I invited her to come to my room and sit down. Then I scribbled on a piece of paper : "Do you know I have never in all my life kissed a girl? Isn't that terrible? What about my kissing you?" I folded it carefully and handed it to her. I was overcome with shyness and yet I wanted to see whether her reaction would give me my answer. As she read the note her expression remained completely neutral, betraying nothing of interest, anger, amusement or affection and just at that moment an American boy came in so any further discussion was made impossible. Then the time came for her to leave. I felt so nervous that I could not bring myself to ask her whether she would return and she left without mentioning it either.

I cursed myself not having taken the initiative earlier and spent the whole morning in a state of nervous tension, my ears alert for her footsteps and eyes perpetually turned towards the door. I began to wish fervently that she had said no, and settled the matter once and for all.

In the afternoon heavy rain began to fall and as evening drew on, I gave up all hope of seeing her that day. But at 8.30 in the evening when I was having my dinner, she suddenly appeared, wearing a cream coloured waterproof, wet with rain. I could not believe my eyes; to come so late was definitely "improper", yet I was filled with a mounting excitement. "What has brought you here at this hour ?"

"Nothing." She seemed abstracted. Conversation continued in a desultory way.

"Why don't you have some coffee ?"

"No, I must leave almost immediately." But she allowed herself to be persuaded and stood, sipping the excellent coffee which the restaurant provided.

"Now, I must run," she said, and moved towards the door.

I jumped up to follow her and then gathering all my courage said quickly : "What about meeting tonight ?"

"When ?"

The question left me speechless with joy. "At eleven thirty !"

"Where ?"

"At Coaker's Walk."

"All right. But I must go now," and she disappeared into the darkness.

The tension of the whole day was relaxed. I was suddenly very happy and the simplicity with which the meeting had been arranged seemed, after all my anxiety, to be very funny. When I returned inside to rejoin my friends I was laughing. "What's the joke ?" they asked. "Oh ! it was only C. She said something very amusing."

I had some difficulty in escaping that night. I had thought everybody would be in bed but someone was drying photograph negatives in the kitchen and everyone else had gathered there in the warmth and was gossipping about the affairs of the day. Time passed and no one made a move. In the end I announced that I was going for a walk. I receive one or two odd looks. It was foggy and raining and no one with any sense would wish to go walking in such weather. I left in a hurry, already later than I had intended.

Kodaikanal was a small place where every one knew every one else. To be seen at eleven o'clock at night making for the Coaker's Walk would have created a great stir, for the place was renowned for its romantic associations. So I took off my spectacles and wrapped my scarf well round the lower part of my face so that only my nose and eyes were visible. I began to run uphill. I was already 15 minutes late and filled with apprehension now that I was outside. Supposing she had turned up in time and finding me not there, left again? It was too awful to contemplate. I walked up the path inside the compound of St. Peter's Church and I looked around. There was no one. My heart sank and I sat down on the steps in utter dejection.

Then I heard footsteps. Thinking that it might be the gardener I leapt up and hid behind the tree. The footsteps came nearer, sounding menacing in the pitch darkness and then—suddenly she was there before me. We sat down on the steps at the church door. The rain had stopped but it was cold and misty.

"Why have we come?" I asked.

"I don't know. You asked me to come." She was completely uncooperative. Since I had taken two vital steps, I somehow hoped that the next step might be hers, but in vain. We must have remained there for another hour and half. "Aren't you feeling cold?" I asked at last.

"A little."

"What about sitting close together then?"

"Yes, what about it?"

I moved along the step until our shoulders were touching.

"You can put your arm around me, if you like," she volunteered.

I hastily complied but having cleared this first obstacle I found that it was not as exciting as I had imagined it would be, probably because she was wearing a rather thick leather jacket. However, it was a real advance and I was kept busy trying to detect my reaction to this momentous event in my life. Yet it was hard to know what was the next step. I decided to try a different line of attack. I began to explain to her in a very devious manner, how difficult I was finding the whole business. I told her how I had set myself a target of so much work and so much study each day. "But I hate getting out of bed these cold mornings though once I have got out of bed, it is so bad. It is same with the cold shower. It is the first plunge which is so unnerving. So many things in life are like that...!" But it was useless. She would not take the hint. After three solid hours in the cold with no further advance, she said she had to get up early next morning and must go home. I could not object, though faced with the prospect of returning still without having kissed. I knew that after the two hundred steps down the hill our paths would separate and my last opportunity would vanish. Arm in arm we set out. As we drew near the place, I felt my heart beating painfully. What could I do? I felt completely paralysed.

"Thank you for coming," I said. We were facing each other holding hands. There was a silence. It was no good. I simply could not bring myself to kiss her. Perhaps something of my agonized indecision showed in my expression, for she leaned forward, gripped me tightly and kissed me on my left cheek. It was as though I had received an electric shock and it left my whole body tingling. Then she let me go and saying goodnight, walked quickly away. I looked after her spellbound. The rain had ceased, the night was cool and I turned for home, elated, whistling and singing on my way. Only later did it occur to me that although I had been kissed, I had not myself done the kissing.

That evening brought it home to me how powerful is the influence of tradition and custom. In spite of my conscious intellectual attitude and real desire to live out my ideas, I was held back as forcibly as if I had been chained. It gave me an inkling of the difficulties facing the Indian people, weighed down by their effort to take their place in the modern world; difficulties, existing not only in the tremendous material obstacles to be overcome, but in the transformation which will be necessary in their entire intellectual outlook and behaviour patterns.

For all our fears we were after all able to continue our meetings and it was in the park one clear moonlit night when I at last achieved my first kiss. For me it was an experience fraught with magic. It was not a passionate embrace but soft and tender—we were caught up in an enchantment of moonlight and murmuring leaves. The world was transfigured and everything seemed new. It was the most beautiful feeling that I had ever had. Could such a feeling be called immoral? Such a thought seemed almost sacrilegious.

Nowadays I often wonder why this relationship which had no complete physical consummation did not bring a sense of frustration and incompleteness. Perhaps the idea of a platonic friendship was firmly ingrained, for it did not worry me, that like modern youth in the western world, we did not sleep together. Yet we were ecstatically happy and dreaded the thought of the separation which must soon come when she was to leave for Europe, for higher studies. Fleeting thoughts of marriage crossed our minds and once or twice we even discussed such an eventuality, but she wanted freedom to be an artist and I wanted freedom "to follow my stars" and somehow our friendship seemed complete in itself. Yet when at last, the ship carrying her away pulled out of the port of Madras, I felt sick, empty and desolate.

Nearly twenty years have passed since that day and during that time we have met on only five occasions. Both of us have married, we correspond rarely but when we do there still remains the same directness, the same affectionate understanding and concern for the other's welfare. The dream of ideal friendship with women, as I had conceived it, could not have been fulfilled in a better way.

Looking back, I see it as the true beginning of my explorations; the point at which I turned away from the rigid conventions of the past with certain amount of confidence, towards a more liberal view of human relationships. I discovered that love brought a depth and richness into the life which nothing else could provide. The pursuit of love seemed to me to be one of the more valid quests in a society, where getting and spending were primary activities for most people.

Six more years were to pass before I met the woman I wanted to marry and another five before I married her.

During the intervening period my previous idea that sex was to be equated with sin underwent a difficult and gradual evolution. I asked myself and my friends : Why should the sex instinct be suppressed unless one was married? The answer came pat : it shows the strength of character—to be steadfast to the point of unnaturalness. If it were indeed an expression of a general strength of character, then I was prepared to admire anyone who was able to practice such a discipline, just as I would a skilled acrobat who was able to perform all kinds of athletic contortions. But those who preached this sexual morality were not always, it seemed to me, so virtuous in other respects. The attitude of mind which condemns pre-marital experience and yet condones the perpetration of such evils as untouchability and the unashamed exploitation that goes on in the Indian families of poorer people like servants, and of unfortunate relations, especially women, was one which was wholly unacceptable to me. Society, I thought had developed a lopsided bed-conscious morality.

I wanted to discover for myself whether sex would enrich life or degrade it; strengthen love or kill it; was a source of happiness or misery; whether I should become a better or worse person by giving free rein to my instincts. I soon discovered that there could be no single answer to these questions; it would differ from one individual to another, according to what he was, and what he wanted to make of sex. I came to the conclusion that matters concerning sex were ethically neutral and that the value of sexual experience was determined by time, circumstances and poeple, rather than by anything inherently good or bad in the experience itself.

So when I come to know a handsome, buxom Punjabi girl in Delhi I was quite clear in my mind what my approach should be.

She was the first girl whom I regarded with a purely human interest. She was quite ordinary and it was an experience for me to sit and listen to her talking of her dreams and frustrations, hear her observations on men and events, without any intervention from any of my external ideas and theories. She shared the saner Punjabi attitude towards sex and was not in the least inhibited about the expression of warm feelings. But loveplay generates a progressive dissatisfaction. My curiosity was boundless, my virginity at the age of twentysix seemed no longer an ornament but a burden, and one warm summer afternoon, she enthusiastic, I, very hot and far too excited to make a success of it, the burden was shed once and for all. I had made the final, conscious break with traditional values. I am certain that I was no worse a person for the experience. I learnt the full extent of what relationship with women could mean and acquired the capacity to respond to them at all levels.

I do not think, however, that unless one ends up in bed one cannot have a meaningful relationship with a woman. Some of happiest of my encounters have been without physical consummation. I tried to cultivate sincerity, a clarity of approach and this, and the efforts to give the best of myself and evoke the best in the other, have left me with a host of memories, which leave a lingering fragrance behind them.

But for marriage, I had painted a vivid picture in my mind; my future wife should have the basic goodness and emotional warmth to be able to have genuine feelings of love; she should have the capacity for complete fulfilment which for me is the finest end to the act of love; she should be able to run a household with a fair amount of efficiency and be capable of earning her own living for it seemed unlikely I should even earn enough to keep us both; she should be deeply interested in the intellectual problems of our time; her prime concern should not be just to maintain an orderly material and social existence, but to create or help in creating something which would be of positive and enduring value to mankind. It was indeed a tall order but I was in search of someone who would at least approximate to these ideas.

I met an English woman a teacher in a class of Modern Philosophy in London who closely resembled my ideal. The love which gradually developed between us was love in all of its dimensions, just as I wanted. I could not imagine being more profoundly involved. "If I never love again," I told her, "this will have been enough." But I was leaving for India. The stage of exploration was ending and the period of commitment about to begin. My life was full of uncertainties and this, combined with difficulties on her side, made marriage out of the question. It seemed tragic that two people who were so close were destined to live apart.

So the years passed and I was engrossed in my work but increasingly I felt the need for loving and being loved in marriage. Three years after I had left England sheer luck took me back there for a brief period, and we met again. It seemed that the years of separation and longing had never been. The future did not matter. Time was short and we were absorbed in ourselves and in the enchantment of the present which was so seen to end. So we parted, this time we thought for the last time and I travelled on into Europe. During the weeks that followed I learnt of the possibility of taking up a post in Vienna. It was a difficult decision; much work started in India would not have first hand attention but the advantages made it seem worth while. I decided to take it and so it came about that we came together once more to spend Christmas among the lights and music and frozen forests of Vienna, one of Europe's most fascinating cities. When Easter came to London, with the parks full of cherry blossom and daffodils, and the air warm with Spring, I crossed the Channel and one sunny day, quietly, almost secretly, we were married.

My long pursuit of love had ended. Yet in a sense it had only just begun, for love grows with knowledge and the practice of love can never be too long. To have known love with all its ecstasy and pain, is to come the closest that man can to what some call God, the highest value. I can understand now why religious people speak of God as love. If ordinary mortals are to realise God, love is the only term of reference within their grasp which can give a maximum sense of value.

I have not known God, but I have known love and it is good to have known it.

CHAPTER II

"Religion is what an individual does with his solitariness."
— Whitehead.

My first doubts about the existence of God came at the age of eleven. One day I went with my family to Tarakeswar, one of the holy places of Bengal, where there are many old temples. In one of these, there was, if I remember rightly, an image of the god in black stone. The room where it was housed was beautifully decorated with flowers and the air was filled with fragrance of incense. We were told that the special significance of this deity was that if the worshipper prayed with his whole heart for the fulfillment of one particular wish then his prayer would be answered. He must not however let the wish be known to anyone, otherwise the efficacy of the prayer would be lost. I immediately knelt down and asked that Mohun Bagan, my favourite football team in Calcutta, should become league champion that year.

During the season I followed the results with doubled enthusiasm but the prayer which I had made so earnestly, (and with, I was certain, my whole heart) was never answered. I was thoroughly disillusioned and became very sceptical of all stories which held any implication of the miraculous and this scepticism affected to some extent, the conventional religious beliefs which I had held until then. For I had believed in God and thought that everything in the universe was ordered according to his command. I thought that a religious person should lead his life according to His will, and that he could draw near to Him through prayer. I took religion seriously and was curious about its precepts, but being born and brought up in a Bengali Hindu family living in a city, it was not surprising that I received no clear instruction at home. Nor did I undergo any religious discipline. Only on one occasion during the year, at the time of the Durga Puja, on the last day when the images were immersed we children were compelled to write with red ink on plantain leaves, "Sri, Sri, Durga sohai . . . ." with the grace of the goddess Durga. This was our only religious compulsion. I never discovered to which of the multitude of Hindu gods I was supposed to have a special attachment. Only when I was grown up, did I come to know quite incidentally, that our family were Saivites, worshippers of Siva. Nobody taught us about the contents of the Hindu scriptures such as the Upanishads or the Bhagavad-Gita. Even our knowledge of the Hindu epics like the Ramayana and Mahabharat was on a popular level and I read them on my own initiative. We were never taught any set prayers.

Yet my parents were not agnostics or sceptical. They were, in fact, quite devout and used to pray daily but they never insisted that we should do the same. Perhaps because I observed their habit and wished to imitate them, I wanted to pray too, but having no prayer I had to compose my own, which centred chiefly round the petition that God should help me to be a well-behaved boy.

Later I wondered why it was, that my parents, although themselves religious, never instructed their children in such matters and found that it was in a way typical of the Hindu attitude, when emphasis is placed on a code of behaviour rather than on doctrine. Much importance is placed on self-realization, the urge for which arises from an inner disquiet, rather than any external pressure. Moreover, since individuals are so different in temperament, intellectual and emotional make-up, the path of realization will also be different. Consequently no particular stress is laid upon a single method or discipline. The result is the bewildering number of gods which are the various manifestations of the universal Godhead, and which represent every possible intellectual interpretation of the universe, from the lowest form of animism to the subtlest forms of metaphysics. There is for this reason, rather more religious tolerance and far less institutionalization of religion in Hinduism than some of the higher religions such as Judaism, Christianity and Islam.

When I joined a Christian Missionary School I found that before classes started the Indian headmaster or the English Rector would begin the day with a prayer. "Our Father which art in heaven. . . ." and the boys would repeat it after in soft murmuring voices. I was very confused. I knew it was not our prayer. After carefully considering the matter I decided that I would not join in with the others and while they were murmuring away, I used to say my own private prayer in Bengali "Hey Bhagaban...." "Oh! God, help me to become a good boy and to do my studies well. Make me respecting to my elders and generous towards my friends..." The prayer would end with the kind of mental offering of "Pronam" during which I folded my hands and raised them to my forehead in attitude of reverance.

Although I realised that Christianity was not my religion I was quite interested in its teaching even at an early age. Hindus believe that in times of troubles or distress in the world, messengers of God or *avatars* are sent and they think of the prophets of other religions as avatars. I was fascinated by the stories of Old and New Testament and had no difficulty at all in accepting Jesus Christ as one of the *avatars*. That did not mean that I found no difference between Christianity and Hinduism. It was one thing to consider Jesus as one of the prophets and another to make him the sole means of salvation for the world and the focus of all one's religious longings and experience.

In retrospect I feel it was a good thing that in my childhood I did not undergo any intense religious "grilling". My ideas, therefore, remained flexible and the renunciation at a later date of the older faith did not leave me with any feelings of guilt nor did the convictions held during my youth continue to obsess me when I had rejected them intellectually.

For some years, however, I still found my religious expression in the belief and rituals of Hindus. Even the visit to Tarakeswar did not completely shatter my faith, although it certainly raised doubts in my mind. Nevertheless I continued to stick to the Hindu code of behaviour, to participate in religious ceremonies and to say my little prayer for virtue at very irregular intervals.

After the even tenor of my life was disturbed by the visit to a village in Bihar, I was urgently looking round, not only for an explanation for the sufferings in the world but for some teaching which would provide a guide to action. But the Hindu idea that the world is Maya, illusion, "a fevered dance of fleeting appearances, which masks the pure reality of uncreated being", was completely unacceptable to me and the theory of *Karma* left me cold. I did though, get much inspiration and enlightenment from the writings of Swami Vivekananda; he seemed so refreshingly different from the average religious person. His social consciousness, his impatience with the poverty and degradation of the Indian people and his strong call to action struck a responsive chord in me and his book "Karma Yoga" is one of the few books which has made real impact on my life.

Religious life in India generally, I found depressing in the extreme. When I came to know people, communities and institutions which called themselves religious the more certain I was that Freud's view was a correct one; that for man, God was the omnipotent father figure, from whom he could obtain comfort in time of trouble. I found men and women asking their *gurus* what would happen about their daughter's marriage, or their son's job or their grandchildren's illness. Religion for them was more often than not the projection of their sense of insecurity in the universe, an expression of their need for a father's protection. Gurus are, in fact, known as "father" and being shrewd psychologists are often able to give advice, or failing that, solace in distress. The majority of devotees I found were deeply engrossed in their material life and wanted to make good and the *gurus* were a help in that process. The whole business seemed to me to have very little to do with spiritual realization.

I also discovered that there was a great deal of truth in Marx's assertion that religion in the "opium of the people." So often I came across apparently intelligent individuals whose reasoning was a process based on faith, tradition and automatic thinking, which would collapse when examined in the light of cold rationality. I found this attitude quite outrageous. The smug acceptance of the status quo in the name of *Karma,* the religious sanction behind the caste system, the unashamed exploitation by the priestly class in every place of pilgrimage I ever visited, completely alienated me from the religion I found in India. Later, in Europe, particularly in Britain, I became convinced that Marx was correct in his contention that religion was a prop for class rule. There I found chief dignitaries in the church not only championing the cause of imperialism in Cyprus but even finding religious justification for atomic war. "Who knows", asked one, "it might be the will of God that the world should end by nuclear fission."

It was Vivekananda who made me realize that it would

be a mistake to throw out the baby with the bath water. Although I disapproved of the psychology behind popular religion and detested the way in which a handful of people, for their own or class interest, exploited the inner fears and anxieties of the common man, that did not automatically turn me towards the acceptance of a materialist philosophy. No philosophy or religion, I thought should be evaluated merely by the inadequacy of its adherents. Nor would the good qualities of its disciples make a particular philosophy intellectually more valid. Any idea to be acceptable has to pass the test of human experience, reason and man's deepest longings. A religion fulfilling all these requirements might yet be professed by rogues and scoundrels but this would not detract from its validity. The significance of Jesus Christ is not to be measured by the wickedness of Popes or the acts of those who burned and tortured in his name.

Disillusionment with conventional religion made me wish to discover what was the real essence of religious thought.

It became clear that religion plays three distinct but inter-related roles. First, it provides a code of behaviour; secondly, it creates in individuals a certain state of mind and finally, it seeks to offer the truth.

Although there are differences relating to diet, marriage laws and the position of women in the ethical codes of the various religions, there is no creed which consciously approves obvious misconduct. There is a general tendency to uphold truthfulness, honesty and love, with the idea of developing individual integrity and social harmony.

The real sources of religious morality are its metaphysics but I found increasingly either that I was unable to understand or that I was incapable of accepting them. Nevertheless I found that it was possible to evaluate whether a particular action was justifiable or not in terms of human experience and history. That love is better than hatred could be proved from a social and psychological point of view, whether or not one accepted the metaphysics of the Buddha or Christ. So I concluded, that at any rate so far as morality was concerned religion had nothing to offer since it was possible to evolve an ethical code which did not have its foundation in metaphysics.

A more subtle function of religion however, is to create a rather special state of mind. A sincere religious belief can instil in the individual a sense of destiny, a feeling that he is a part of a vast and mysterious design created by God. Such a belief not only endows man with a consciousness of identity with the world around him but often inspires him with great will and purpose, sometimes almost superhuman in its strength. Moreover, the faith that life exists beyond death provides consolation when he is overcome with grief for the loss of those he loves. And when facing death man often has an overwhelming urge to believe in something which transcends individual mortality. I have known people who denied the existence of God all their lives, try to seek him when they are about to die.

I remember asking a leader of the Young Communist League in the Soviet Union what method they employed in their anti-religious propaganda. He replied that they attempted to convince the people that everything in the universe happened according to natural law, and without the intervention of the divine will. Now, even if one were intellectually convinced that the universe is a natural phenomenon, the outcome of some quite accidental movement of atoms through space, psychological factors in religion cannot fail to exercise a profound influence over the majority of people. The urge in man to know and to seek his fate in the universe will continue to give religion its power over his life, whatever the materialists may say.

The feeling of identification with others of the same community of belief, which religion gives, has both its positive and negative sides. In its worst form it generates a sense of exclusiveness and parochialism often amounting to arrogance. One of the most tragic results has been the communalism which has grown up between the Hindu and Muslim communities causing unspeakable savageries to be committed in the name of religion.

In a more positive way it can however help individuals to emerge from their isolated selves and take their place in a society of like-minded people.

The peculiar state of mind brought about by religion is something which is very satisfying to some people. For my mother praying in the corner of a dark room in the evening, prayers bring peace and tranquility. But the Fifth Symphony of Beethoven can likewise arouse in me wonderful feeling of being transported beyond the mundane world. Is it possible to say that one state of mind is superior to another? At best I can say that I am not interested in attaining emotional satisfaction in her way, but since I have never in fact had such a "religious" experience, it would be impossible for me to pass a considered judgment. What value have these subjective feelings? They can be evoked in a great variety of ways by narcotics and drink, by music and dancing, by the sight of a beautiful woman or a wonderful sunset, by great art or the excitement of speed, by yogic exercises and prayer. The strong appeal which such mental (or spiritual) states have for a great many people is unquestionable. The nature of such feelings remains largely unexplained and this particular aspiration in man, to attain to some realm of being beyond his earth-bound self is one much feared by all the "engineers of human soul" because once in the grip of these fascinations man's behaviour becomes unpredictable and is no longer controllable by reason. The "engineers" would like to abolish them, if they could. Yet what kind of world would it be where the whole range of aesthetic delights, emotional intensities, sensual pleasures and temporary self-forgetfulness have been banished for ever, because they do not promote the immediate social good or individual usefulness?

Are there any objective criteria by which the quality of such sensations can be judged? It is extremely difficult to make any hard and fast rules and yet one might, on the basis of psychological insight, say categorically that alcoholism or drug-addiction are the manifestation of mental instability and weakness. What then should be our attitude towards the mental states aroused by such a drug as mescalin, which according to Aldous Huxley opens "the doors of perception" in such a way that it results in the more immediate and splendid apprehension of reality than we can ever know in our day to day existence? Do they have any validity or are they a kind of hallucination?

And what of all the multitude of delights and ecstacies experienced through the various forms in which religious faith is expressed? People respond to these in so many ways; through an attraction to the dialectics of theology and metaphysics, through the beautiful symmetry of religious architecture and sculpture, through the sensual delights of music and painting, through rituals and pageantry of religious festivals. I have found that, although of an analytical and questioning bent of mind, I have often been affected in an inexplicable way by the aesthetic aspects of religion. I am still haunted by the ethereal, unearthly music which I heard echoing through the emptiness of a Serbian church in Belgrade. I can understand why men and women sit for hours in the cool gloom of a church, finding solace in this interlude away from the world. It satisfies a peculiar urge in man which can find fulfilment neither in the absorption in one's private life, nor in energetic social action, nor in addiction to wine and women, nor in intellectual or aesthetic pursuits : the urge to grapple with one's solitariness.

At one time I used to practice yogic exercises regularly, and found that I frequently was transported into the most exquisite moods of happiness and delight; moods generated not by any events outside but by something within myself. I felt simple joy, without being aware of the cause and became actutely conscious of myself and of the pleasure of being alive. Yet paradoxically, as when in moments of great happiness one sometime wishes that one could die, so these moods induced a disinterest in external life. Even when I compelled myself to emerge from the spell, there remained an overpowering urge to return to the state of bliss.

From these rudimentary experiences I came to understand two things. Firstly, that when people renounce all those material things which ordinary mortals desire, to adopt religious life, I think it is this kind of delight which could sustain them in a condition of prolonged asceticism and denial. Secondly, the fact that this state of mind is valued so highly makes one see everything also in relation to it. Anything which promotes the enchantment is good; that which frustrates its development is bad or unimportant.

However, except for those *yogis* who go consciously into *samadhi* not to come back to life again, others return to normal consciousness and are subjected to all the laws of nature and have to adjust to them in order to survive. For myself, I found that practical efficiency and the cultivation of yogic discipline were incompatible. Intellectually I was convinced that a balance was possible but at that time since it caused "absent-mindedness" in a job which entailed remembering the minutest details of administration, I had consequently to abandon the practice.

One lasting effect which the experience had was that I have retained a memory of the "goodness" I felt. A general feeling of well-being made me have a more positive approach to other people. Whether or not these attitudes already existed in me and were filtered and strengthened in this way or whether entirely new feelings could emerge with the practice of yoga is difficult to say.

If one considers only the delights and ecstasies which religious experiences can cause, without thinking whether they provide insight into reality or increase the efficiency in human beings, Hindu religion has much to offer. It is said that *samadhi* produces symptoms somewhat similar to orgasm. If after disciplined exercises it is possible to attain samadhi for half an hour, it will not be surprising if those who reach that stage are wildly excited about it!

In the advanced, industrial societies which the West has already attained and towards which we in India are steadily moving, the average man is confronted by a wide range of activities which are gradually tending to push the previous interest in religion into the background. One can see the advance of a secular society, where the arts, music and recreation of all kinds fully occupy leisure hours and leave no time for contemplation or the cultivation of an inner quietude. It would seem that religion is fighting a losing battle, especially among the younger generation and it is certain that among young people in every country there is a reaction against the conservative dogmas which religions have preached for centuries. This may only be a temporary manifestation of new ideas and ideals, or it may become a permanent attitude. It does seem however, that with a more liberal education, and the wider contacts now possible, as travel becomes quicker and cheaper, many of the barriers and antagonisms which were built up by religions will gradually become a thing of the past.

The ultimate validity of religion lies in the question whether it offers "truth" or not. This raises two questions: is there a spiritual reality beyond the material world that we perceive through our senses and if there is such a reality how can it be apprehended?

Nineteenth century physics could confidently rule out any possibility of the existence of spiritual reality. Twentieth century physics is much more imprecise about material reality. The once fixed and solid atom has dissolved into radiation and consequently room is left for a certain amount of speculation with idealistic implications. As Sir James Jeans said, "In general, the universe seems to be nearer a great thought than a great machine." Physics however says nothing about the existence of spiritual reality but one can conclude that since physics makes no definite assertion about the nature of such reality, then it is possible to examine the problem from other angles.

The first question that arises in my mind is : with all that we know about our world can we say that the evolution of matter, through life and mind, to the consciousness of values is a part of a mechanical process combined with certain "accidents"? Or, can one discern a pattern in the series of "accidents"? With the present state of knowledge we cannot give any answer. Such a pattern is "conceivable" but not "knowable"—unless one knows definitely how it is caused. To suggest that some sort of "force" is trying to unfold itself through nature by an evolutionary process would not be far-fetched.

All the religions assert that through an intellectual process one can reach only a certain point in the path of knowledge; in order to grasp "true" knowledge, which can provide a key to the mysteries of reality, the intuitive process is necessary. Radio provides a useful analogy here. I can sit in my room and strain my ears to the utmost to hear broadcasts being made from the Calcutta radio station about five miles away. I can hear nothing and might say therefore that no broadcasts are being made.

Only if I have an instrument which catches the sound waves can I hear the speech and music as clearly as if it were next door. The Vedantist would say that every human being has within himself such an instrument which lies dormant but which can with conscious yogic efforts be made sensitive so that we become aware of the many of the aspects of reality which we would ordinarily miss. Sri Ramakrishna once said to Vivekananda that God was more "real" to him than Vivekananda himself. It is through such intuitive knowledge that a direct experience of spiritual reality is supposed to be possible.

I have known personally a number of people who say that

in moments of exceptional awareness they have been conscious of the actual presence of God. Now assuming that this is true, this experience, like all subjective knowledge, must remain their exclusive possession. However vividly mystics might attempt to translate their knowledge into words, for others, it will still be a second hand, verbal description. As Sri Ramakrishna said: "God cannot be touched by tongue." It is only when we experience ourselves that we can decide whether the knowledge gained has meaning or validity for us.

The fact that there exists a process of knowledge outside the normal channels of the senses, is being gradually accepted by scientific opinion. The pioneering work of Dr. Rhine and others in the field of extra-sensory perception has made an important contribution in this type of research. The evidence for the functioning of such a faculty of the human mind is strong and full acceptance of the fact would bring about a veritable revolution in our conception of knowledge. If the gap between the intellectual and the intuitive processes could be bridged, man would be on the threshold of a new phase of his development.

Julian Huxley (who is by no means a religious man in the conventional sense) speculating on the future of man on the occasion of Darwin's centenary said that perhaps the most significant evolutionary change in the future would be the extension to ordinary individuals of the ability to acquire knowledge intuitively. Sri Aurobindo expressed a similar conviction when he said that the intuitive capacity which is now confined to a few mystics and artists will, at some future date, become within the capability of the average human being. If such prophecies materialise then intuitive experience would become a part of social knowledge and not the intimate, personal knowledge which they are at present.

However, it is argued that the validity of a universal spiritual reality is exemplified by the striking similarity in the experience of the mystics of various countries, ages and religions. Unless there were some objective Existence or Being how can these strange resemblances be explained? It is certainly a powerful argument and must inevitably cut across the exclusive claims of different religions to be the sole purveyors of truth.

It seems to me that the real task of all religions is to enable their adherents to be able to apprehend truth directly at its source. Every religion began with the mystical vision of a prophet or a teacher and it should be the goal of every one of his followers to experience reality for himself. All else is irrelevant and the persistent interest of intelligent people in dogma, theology and metaphysics is something I have failed to understand. To me it seems nothing more than a useless spinning of words.

For centuries now religion has been encumbered by its association with so many non-religious aspects of life, with the affairs of the State, with politics, with high finance, with morality and education. The uneven struggle between science and religion and the increasing influence of scientific thought is putting religion progressively into the background. This cleansing process is, and will continue to be, beneficial. It will send those who claim to be religious directly to the real essence of their faith—the mystical experience.

In this manifestation of religion I am deeply interested. No relinquishing of rationality is involved. In fact, the apprehension of reality through the intuitive process could be a part of the scientific quest for truth. To arrive at some definite conclusion in this sphere of knowledge is one of the intellectual passions of my life.

Until I can claim to have done this however, on the question of religious experience my mind will continue to remain open.

Because of this attitude I do not feel hostile to the deep and essential elements of India's spiritual tradition. I have the feeling that something of vital importance to modern man may come out of it and for that, people trained in modern scientific outlook may benefit from the search of "secret India."

Chapter III

"Follow what the heart desires without transgressing what is right." — Confucius.

During my childhood days my conduct was determined by two main factors—a disposition to imitate the elders and the necessity for submission to imposed discipline. Slowly I learnt that it was considered wrong to use dirty words, to have brawls, to tell lies, to steal, to smoke, to brush my hair in a stylish way and to be disobedient to those older than myself. Later on I had impressed upon me the evils of drink, of eating beef and of expressing myself in any way by the impulses of sex.

The concept of the 'good life' was clear. You had to pass examinations with credit; secure a good job in order to obtain as high a standard of living as possible; your parents would then find you a suitable girl of your own caste to marry; and when you had children you should look after them and try to build a house for your family, which would stand as a visible symbol of your worldly achievement. At last with a host of children and grand children gathered around you saying the words of God, you would die peacefully in your bed. 'He made a good death' everyone would say. If you did not succeed in achieving these ambitions, still this glowing picture would remain at the back of your mind, a constant reminder of what might have been.

Apart from the fact that when I was young my desire to be learned was given first priority, over and above the acquisition of wife, family and wealth, my concept of the good life very much coincided with the generally accepted one.

As I have said, I was thought to be a good boy in those days : this meant that I possessed a negative kind of goodness. I did not do this, I did not do that. This inability to do bad things was, I suspect, part of my lethargic nature, rather than any positive pursuit of virtue, and I have not been able to decide whether it was these inactive propensities which drove me to the habit of reading, or whether the craze that I developed for reading, numbed my faculties, to the extent of making me quite indifferent to many of those things which most people get excited about.

From this soft, easy-going approach to life, quite in keeping with the environment in which I grew up, I was suddenly made aware of an alien world of misery and deprivation where complacency seemed downright wicked and the acceptance of the conventional "good life" an indication that some awareness, some sensitivity must be lacking. I began to hate the indifference and indolence of mind which was apparent everywhere. People lived with their senses, intelligence and imagination inert towards matters which seemed to be important, and at the same time devoted precious years to the pursuit of trivialities. Wordsworth had made his point, it seemed :

"Getting and spending we lay waste our powers,
We have given our hearts away, a sordid boon...."

How does it happen, this waste, this atrophy of human potentialities? It is one of the most intriguing aspects of the personality. One of the best definitions of education I have found is that it helps us to see things in their correct proportion. This is only possible I think, when we are aware of the real context of our living in relation to our family and friends, school, language, culture, country, the world, nature and the universe itself. As a general rule our awareness in the deepest sense of the term, does not extend beyond the narrow limits of the world made up of our home and workplace and those associated with these places. Outside these our interest becomes 'detached.' We are not moved by events in the next street, village, town or in a distant country. Even if we are, our knowledge is generally superficial and our reactions are transitory in character. We can perhaps discuss such matters, often with unpardonable ignorance, but they do not really affect us deeply or have any impact on our lives. In the 'outside' world everything seems tolerable or permissible. Formerly most people had some idea of an absolute in the realm of morals and even if they could not maintain this, at least they were conscious of a 'fall from grace.' Even then, their attitude was basically a negative one : cheating was wrong; bribery was wrong; running away with your friend's wife was wrong. There was little conception of a more positive and active concern about one's neighbour. Provided one did not do him positive harm, everything could be all right. This attitude of accepting things as they are and rationalising them, I found thoroughly inadequate : I became interested in what people did, rather than in what they did not do.

I do not know how I was able to break up the crust which envelopes an individual and his sensibilities, preventing him from communicating with the outside world in a total and uninhibited manner, so that some meaning and purpose are given to his life. As it was, my visit to the village in Bihar resulted in "an extension of the ethical impulse from the restricted individual and family sphere to the domain of human activity" (Ignazio Silone). My enlarged vision was like a miracle to me. Suddenly it mattered very much that some people were so poor that they did not even get two square meals a day, that their children had no opportunity for education, that medical and health services were almost totally absent, that they lived in disgusting and insanitary conditions, that they were ignorant and superstitious.

Only action which was relevant to the central problem; only behaviour or aspiration in an individual which either directly or indirectly sought to find solutions to the problem, seemed worthwhile to me.

Earlier in this book I have tried to analyse in a cursory way why this "miracle" happened to me and yet did not affect my brother and sister who were with me at the time. There has been much controversy in the scientific world concerning the relative influence on the individual of heredity and environment. What is the mysterious nucleus in a personality which, even when subjected to the same environmental and hereditary influence, causes it to register a quite different reaction to a given stimulus? Did I respond differently because of some quality of imagination or compassion which was present in my nature and not in that of the others? I have suggested that perhaps I felt sympathy in the presence of sorrow because I had known sorrow myself. Does this mean that unless I have experienced pain myself then I shall be incapable of reacting to the pain in others in a positive way? Or, will an inherent sensitivity and imagination enable me to identify myself with the suffering of others without having personally experienced it? Can such important qualities of character be instilled by education and upbringing?

I once asked Prof. A. J. Ayer, a noted British philosopher of the Logical Positivist school (which asserts that it is not the task of philosophy to deal with the problems of value) how he made his own personal value-judgments. He replied: "From my temperament." This theory was completely new to me and sounded so irrational that I contested it. Later I came to see that, although it has an unpleasant ring of 'fatalism' about it, there is a considerable amount of truth in what he said.

This particular incident in Santhal Parganas, experienced by the three of us, was transmuted in different ways according to our 'temperaments', diverse experiences and our interpretation of these experiences. Out of these three different components only the activity of learning to interpret events can be a conscious and controllable process.

My own response seemed to have had an almost determinist pattern. My temperament and the nature of past events, which were an integral part of that response were completely outside my control.

Once I had been so deeply affected, the impossibility of settling again to my earlier easy acceptance of conventional values, of living life at a lower intensity, made it urgent for me to find a new equilibrium. I was moved to act by an inner compulsion which, though it might have been justified intellectually was not therefore any less powerful.

My youthful psychological problem could well have been summed up as being the result of the inferiority complex. Why I chose to identify myself with the fate of unknown millions rather than find a solution in the self-aggrandisement beneath which many afflicted in this way hide their feelings, it is difficult to say. Did the deliberate pursuit of an inconspicuous death, the development of a kind of martyrdom complex mean that after my visit to the village, life had become even more intolerable than before? Did there lie behind all my brave thoughts and words of heroism a lurking fear of life itself? I do not know.

Yet certainly the path I chose was quite inimical to my character or temperament. Basically I was a solitary, and life in politics meant constant association with people. I believed in directness, and politics demanded diplomatic skill. I preferred a quiet, studious life and political action involved an enormous amount of physical work.

Despite all these, I deliberately set my face in the direction of the political jungle. The impetus was clearly emotional, but the intellectual processes at work helped in clarifying the issues and in modifying and directing a life of action, which I would not 'naturally' have chosen.

It is in fact only when our strongest feelings are affected that we attain to that pitch of vivid realization which is the fountainhead of all authentic values. Without such feelings a favourable environment and good education will fall like seeds by the wayside, which send down only shallow roots which are soon chocked by the weeds which grow up in profusion about them. In such circumstances confrontation with real 'temptations' uproots the personality and one becomes a conventional and conformist individual, good enough for the smooth functioning of society but useless as a catalyst for its quickening and growth.

Everything which is of value to human civilization and culture has grown out of the restlessness and disquiet of the human spirit combined with the intelligence and sustained labour of man. These efforts by which he has forged his way from a primitive existence to unimaginable heights of scientific, artistic and humane achievement need no special pleading to prove that they are ethically good. Yet are these creative potentialities common to all men? Does every one possess within himself the vision to see a world ahead of his time and the drive to move towards it?

Children, it is true, are often remarkable for their clarity of thought and perception, but how soon their eyes become clouded, their originality dimmed! The adult frequently finds it difficult to 'take off' from a purely animal existence of survival, security and sex, despite the subtle dissatisfaction with which his mind is afflicted. How can the child's insatiable curiosity for life be maintained and the sharp youthful intensity preserved? How can the dormant spirit be awakened? Is the desire to transcend oneself an endowment possessed only by a few individuals? And is the failure to fulfil an early promise simply the result of the fact that to climb is more difficult than to descend? How are those who live to the full extent of their capacities impelled? From where comes their inspiration and how are they able to maintain a simple clarity of values in the midst of such conflicting and confusing situations?

There can be no universal answer. For some perhaps there is a moment of revelation which even afterwards is the guiding principle of their lives; for others it is the result of an act of will determined by "uncontrollable" temperament or event. Perhaps the action of the will has been given impetus by an inspiring leader, a teacher or a comrade.

For most people there arises the question: why should I trouble myself about the problems I have not created? Is not the burden of my near relations enough for me to carry? I derive pleasure from helping my friends in distress. Is this not enough? Why should I care about anything which does not directly concern me, my family and friends, especially since I, as an individual, am almost powerless to affect the course of larger events in the world? With what valid objection can one counter such an attitude?

In the first place it always seems to me that man does an injustice to himself in depriving his nature of the opportunity for its fullest expression. The average man, leading an "average" life, who might have asked these questions, is only making a very limited use of his faculties. His true potentialities lie dormant. Evolution has provided him with abilities and intellect which do not exist in the vegetable and animal world. Does not each plane of existence—vegetative, animal and human—have its corresponding values? Man's awareness of his environment, of death, his capacity for thought and imagination, his conception of a level of experience which lies outside the solidly material, his consciousness of value, all mean that he has developed a mode of behaviour far in advance of anything in the animal kingdom. Is not the pursuit of values—not directly related to one's survival, security and sex—a basically human quality? Do we not call those men great who have given their lives for the achievement of some values in the realm of truth, beauty or goodness? Even those who think themselves very ordinary are sometimes assailed by a nagging dissatisfaction of mind, which they would find it difficult to define or account for.

We are all of us inheritors. From the treasure-house of the past has been handed down the cultural wealth of every age and clime. We would criticise a man who squandered the accumulated wealth of his fathers but how many of us utilise our human inheritance? Only a very small minority.

Not all of us, of course, have an equal capacity to utilize this knowledge and experience. Variations in man's abilities are accepted facts of biology. Even if everyone gives of his best, there will be considerable variation in the result. We can never all be 'equal' in that sense. But what really counts from the individual's point of view is what efforts have been made rather than what has been achieved.

Any society can be judged by the extent to which it can provide the largest number of people with the opportunity to fulfil their potentialities in this pursuit of worthwhile objectives of truth, beauty and goodness. The best society is that where every single member has an equal chance to achieve this end.

Today more than half the world's population is so much ground down by poverty that they have neither the time nor the strength for anything but the grim struggle for existence. The concept of social, economic and political equality among nations and peoples is, however no longer an utopian dream but a practical possibility, but until this has been brought about, the physical and mental ills, the blind apathy and degradation which spring from poverty, and the artificial class divisions which perpetuate it, are evils against which the entire resources of society and man should be mobilized.

For each man to realize himself through the fullest exercise of his potentialities, without consciously causing ill to another and to live in harmony with his neighbour, seems to me the basis of a moral life and needs no religious sanction.

Admittedly this view is strongly individualistic but when god is dead, when ideologies have been perverted, and the clouds of nuclear war threaten, what else is more real than the consciousness of the self? My own thoughts, desires, sensations and feelings remain as immediate, tangible and irrefutable data even when everything else that I have valued has turned into dust and ashes. Any truly moral life in our time has, therefore, to start from the individual to make it authentic and it cannot be superimposed from the outside. The mind of man has become too sceptical to accept anything at its face value for any length of time.

Moreover, whatever I do, whether it be motivated by the loftiest intentions, or the crudest of self-interest, I cannot escape from the circle of self-satisfaction, unless I am able to abolish the consciousness of self altogether, which level of spiritual development can be attained by only a few and that also, only momentarily.

The desire for self-expression in an age of disintegrating values may often be perverted into negative or destructive action. This is all the more likely to happen in a society where a large number of people feel a strong sense of frustration. Yet the immorality of certain patterns of behaviour clearly emerges when they are viewed in the context of history. It cannot be denied on the basis of historical evidence that in the long run truth and charity are better than lies and hatred, that the Buddha played a more creative role than Ghenzis Khan. Therefore, I consider that history is the second most valuable source of morality in our time.

Man is not only the product of his own nature. He is also the outcome of a process of interaction between his nature and his environment. He is a social being. That is why "Each human being who has only himself for aim suffers from a horrible void" (Andre Gide). Dissociation from environment and the retreat into the isolation of one's self brings madness unless of course it is consciously done in the pursuit of some creative endeavour. To be able to adapt oneself to society as much as possible without abandoning one's individuality and one's struggle against the ills in the society is the third essential task of moral life.

As to the quality of moral life itself, I would agree with Martin Buber that it is to be measured by the depth and number of I-and-Thou relationships established with other persons, situations and ideas—that is, our ability to come into real and direct communication with the whole of our being with the world around us. This attitude of identification makes one tremendously alive. An approach which avoids superficialities and goes directly to the heart of the matter gives an entirely different taste to living. To really to listen to others, to know them, to find a medium for the expression of one's deeper feelings and aspirations is to know real joy. All this, of course, is ancient wisdom but it has to be personally felt and realized in order to make it an effective principle in one's own life.

Such depth of realization cannot of course be attained in an unlimited way. One has to choose. I chose social action to alleviate human suffering because this is the thing in my life which has affected me the most. By this commitment I live. It has made me to see clearly the basic unity of life; every thing is related with every thing else in an unbroken chain. Because of this link events in such far away places as South Africa or Angola, America or the USSR, Vietnam or Cambodia, Cuba or Korea become part of my existence. There is a universal human reality which cuts across the boundaries of countries, language and culture, which lies beneath the superficialities of everyday life. Gradually, for me at least, the desire grew to extend the highest values I had known to society everywhere. My country—right or wrong—is to me an outdated idea. By objective principle all countries have to be judged. My country can be no exception to it.

Having realized the importance of self-expression in my pursuit of diverse experience and knowledge, I soon came to the conclusion that in our society many of the taboos which govern our behaviour are quite meaningless. Because they were imposed and we were expected to accept them without question—my immediate reaction was to defy the conventions simply because they were imposed. The question that my moral self posed related to this aspect of life was not 'why' but 'why not'? Yet such an attitude although comparatively easy to adopt intellectually often involved considerable emotional conflict. I have already described in a previous chapter how this affected me when I came into intimate personal contact with a girl.

Another of the taboos, of all those who belong to Hindu families are made aware of early in their lives, is that against eating beef. Consequently when one of my brothers invited me to a restaurant in Calcutta to partake of this forbidden dish, I readily agreed. It was all verv well, I thought, to admit that cows, bulls and bullocks were very useful animals but to set them up as gods to be worshipped was sheer nonsense. Moreover, viewing the subject from a purely economic point of view it seemed obvious that if the cattle population of India were drastically reduced, those which remained could be better cared for than the scraggy miserable creatures which are seen amongst the garbage and filth of Calcutta streets.

I had on one occasion attended an exhibition held by the Cow Protection League, sponsored by a Hindu communalist organization. At the exit some volunteers were presenting the visitors with a petition to sign against cow slaughter. When I was asked to sign, I refused. "Are you not a Hindu ?", they demanded.

"My parents are Hindus but for economic reasons I am for cow slaughter. If in your opinion one of the criteria for being a Hindu is to be against it then I must admit that I am not a Hindu."

In spite of this however when the beef delicacy was placed before me, I regarded it very dubiously, and felt extremely reluctant to begin the meal. I was annoyed with myself for these irrational feelings but was not prepared to yield to them, thinking that such an action would expose the shallowness of my cherished progressive and radical views.

I put the first piece in my mouth. Only a valiant effort of self-control prevented my spitting it back on to the plate! I gulped and quickly cut a few more pieces and forced myself to swallow them. Then I hurriedly pushed away the plate.

"How do you like the taste ?" asked my brother.

"It's all right but I am not really hungry", I protested.

After this unpromising beginning I gradually became accustomed to the idea and now a well-grilled steak is one of the tastiest dishes I can think of.

The same difficulties faced me when I drank wine for the first time. I was curious to know what it was about drinking which made it such a popular way of passing the time with so many people. I purposely made myself drunk to see what visionary delights resulted from an advanced state of intoxication. I felt terrible, but later realised a modest consumption of wine can create a delightful feeling.

The violation of taboos never resulted in my having any sense of guilt. Yet neither do I think that without drinking wine or eating beef life cannnot be fulfilled. I can well do without either but now if I wish to be a teetotaller or vegetarian it will be a conscious decision based on experience and not on an imposed set of values. This makes all the difference in the world.

Thus it was that I arrived at the point where I had released myself from senseless taboos, grown out of my dependence on family support and achieved intellectual autonomy. I had evolved an ethical approach which combined self-expression with social good and I had vowed to combat the irrationalities and superstitions which I saw all around me. I felt well fortified to hold my ground against any attack and also to be ready to propagate my sense of values.

Then suddenly all the confidence that I had built up through the years collapsed like a house of cards.

I read Sir James Jeans' "The Mysterious Universe". I read of the unimaginable vastness of space, the immense range of geological time. Everything that I had previously thought and known dwindled into insignificance, and life seemed empty of any meaning or purpose. One day this earth would be nothing more but another burnt out star. All the finest achievements of man would come to the same end as the worst crimes he has perpetrated. So why bother about anything? All was futile and meaningless. This arising in the morning from sleep, going through all the repetitive chores of life, to return again to sleep, only to rise once more in an endless cycle of days, which will end only in death. In the context of infinite time, my sixty, seventy years are but the twinkling of an eye. How could there be any meaning or purpose in such a existence? I could find none. Every moment that passed was pushing me inexorably nearer to the abyss into which everyone falls in the end. There was no other path in life except the one which led to death, *my* death.

It seemed to me that the most logical thing in life would be to end it. Yet I wanted to believe that there was some ultimate purpose in existence. I wanted to believe that we continue in some form after we were dead. I wanted to think that every living thing was fulfilling some vast and mysterious divine purpose. But where was the evidence? There seemed to be a wealth of speculation and conjecture yet none was convincing. However, the effort to find an answer to this question provided some kind of justification for continuing life. For whatever the reason, may be fear of death, or an instinctive clinging to life, I have not turned my hand against myself. I am still here, a living, breathing being. Breathing is an assertion of life, an unconscious activity for most people. Yet during a violent attack of asthma I make efforts almost beyond endurance to bring enough air into my lungs to keep myself alive. By breathing I commit myself to life. If I breathe then I must breathe good air, unpolluted by smog or radio-active fall-out. Then automatically I am going to need many other things—water, food and clothing, a house, books, medical care. So my incapacity to end my life commits me willy nilly to many aspects of living whether I like it or not.

I shall want to know love in all its manifestations; love of my family, of my friends, of the woman I have married, of the world about me. I want to live completely and intensely every precious moment. Yet I find no cosmic significance in all this. Although during some intense moments of love or knowledge I feel that some limited and passing significance is thereby imparted to life.

It became apparent to me that I had been drawing unknowingly towards the concept of "Karma Yoga"—which holds that "You have the right to work and not to the fruits thereof." My justification for this attitude was different from that of conventional Hindu metaphysics. I seek no fruit because of the ultimate meaninglessness of life as I understand it now. What little meaning I have found in concrete living drives me to the conclusion that "Fellowship is life and the lack of fellowship is death" (William Morris).

Around this idea the whole of future civilization and culture can be constructed and I shall find fulfillment if I feel that I have been able to make some contribution towards that end.

Chapter IV

> "I am a part of all that I have met.
> Yet all experience is an arch wherethro'
> Gleams that untravell'd world, whose margin fades
> Forever and forever when I move." — Tennyson.

As I grew up there was one thing that I desired with passionate intensity! It was to visit Europe. This ambition was common among many of my friends at that time and existed in spite of the loathing we had for British imperialism and all that it stood for. Guarded and unvoiced suspicions that western civilization might be superior to anything that we could offer, impelled us to make every effort to put it to the test : to plunge ourselves headlong into occidental experience. This equivocal attitude—our rejection of colonialism on the one hand, and our readiness to accept our own inferiority on the other, resulted in a painful ambiguity of thought and feeling which still persists among those who have lived under British rule.

Generally speaking, there were three broad groups of people, typifying the different attitudes towards western ways and ideas. There were those who rejected the whole system, lock, stock and barrel; others who accepted everything uncritically and a third group who felt that the happiest solution would be a synthesis of the best in both societies. I felt myself most in sympathy with this last view and longed to experience at first hand as much as I could of life in Europe. Europe! the fountainhead of modern civilisation and culture, then only known to me from books and travellers' tales; its present unfolding India's dream of the future.

So I started to save money, enough to make a 'grand tour' lasting for a year. In that time I hoped to see sufficient to clarify my ideas and to get to know the feeling of living in the West. After a little over a year I thought I had enough funds to make preparations to leave. I was lucky. The restrictions which later clamped down on tourism had not then come into force. I easily obtained a passport and left Calcutta for Madras, from where I was to fly to Ceylon. I had escaped the net!

The journey had begun. But three years, not one, were to pass before I once more set foot on Indian soil.

Colombo was tense; as though at any moment something would snap, like a too tight violin string. It was in 1956 and an inflammable situation existed between Indians and Ceylonese. In spite of this I managed two days of sight seeing. I liked Colombo. It was a neat orderly city, freshened by the sea-wind, and I should have liked to remain there longer, and seen more of the notable places in Ceylon, but my boat was due to leave for Europe.

The next seven days spent on the French vessel *Henri Poincare* bound for Marseilles were the worst days of my life. The monsoon had broken and the Arabian Sea was in its blackest and most terrifying mood, tossing the ship about like a place of driftwood. I was sick until I thought that I should die. I had one consuming desire to be able to take a small piece of food into my stomach and digest it. Too weak to move, I lay in utter dejection and misery and prayed for an hour's respite from the incessant pitching and tossing. The moment when I awakened one morning from a nightmare of endless days and nights, to find that the rolling had stopped, was one I shall never forget. It was dawn, when for the first time during the voyage I went up on deck to see a clear, cold, light rising out of the sea. Some French soldiers returning from Indo-China were singing a slow rhythmic chorus. The sun rose suddenly, setting fire to the ocean, dispelling the gloom of seven dreadful days.

Within a few hours we were in Djibouti, capital of what was then French Somaliland. Still feeling weak but determined not to miss an opportunity of seeing a part of the African continent, I went with fellow passengers to explore the town. In spite of modern buildings which were springing up everywhere, the great poverty was evident, even to an Indian, who is accus-to seeing it all around him.

In Port Said, which we touched next, one could immediately feel the physical nearness of Europe. There were a larger number of fair skinned people in western dress and the side-walk cafes resembled those I had seen in pictures of European towns. As the ship moved away from the quay I caught sight of the great bulk of the statue of Ferdinand de Lessep facing northwards. Little did we guess that within a few months, when the Israeli-British-French attack was launched on Egypt, that statue, a symbol of Western Power in the Middle East, would be toppled to the earth.

After the churning chaos of the Arabian Sea, the voyage to Marseilles had a dream like quality. Day followed day, of blue sky and blue sea, fading gently into soft moonlit nights. I had made friends on board who were also travelling to Europe for the first time. The warm days were ravelled with our talk which often continued into the early hours.

Then at last the blue hills of Southern Italy appeared on the horizon—my first sight of Europe! I felt a mounting excitement. We sailed on through the narrow straits between Italy and Sicily. Night fell and a million lights danced from either shore. On we sailed through the darkness until in the greyness of dawn we saw the southern coast of France appearing and disappearing in eddies of sea-mist.

Marseilles itself had nothing particularly remarkable to recommend it, but I was amazed at the number of cars, the shops filled with attractive goods, crowded restaurants and side-walk cafes and the generally clean state of the town in comparison with Indian cities. Nowhere could I see what I considered a really poor person. There were numbers of strikingly beautiful women, (though I never grew accustomed to the way in which they breathed garlic all over me). It was sometime before I was used to seeing white people everywhere and since I had been accustomed to thinking of Europeans as *burrasahibs,* it was strange to see them now performing menial tasks.

It was summer time. I sat by the sea and watched the traffic passing at what seemed a crazy, breakneck speed. Nobody seemed to have a moment to lose. Clearly life moved with a different rhythm from life in India. I was in Europe! It was like beginning a new book—I wanted to cut the pages quickly and discover what new knowledge was hidden inside.

From Marseilles I travelled by express through the beautiful countryside to Paris. There I lay on my bed on a tiny pension revelling in my good fortune. Millions dream of seeing Paris but for few such dreams are ever realised. My private ecstasy was suddenly interrupted by a loud roaring sound; the bed shook violently. An earthquake, I thought, expecting to see the walls crumbling around me any minute. Then the sound died away, the vibrations ceased. So I was not to die on my first day in Paris after all! It dawned on me what had happened; the pension was built over the Metro and the trains passed below the ground under my room every few minutes.

I spent the next few days exploring the city; ascending the Eiffel Tower to see the river Seine threading its sinuous way beneath the famous bridges; walking down the wide Champs Elysees towards the Arc de Triomphe. Behaviour was much less inhibited here, I thought. The public kissing and necking amazed me; even to hold hands or link arms in Calcutta would cause raised eyebrows, but here there seemed to be no limits.

Paris is a city of treasures and spent hours in the Louvre delighting in the sight of masterpieces of which I had previously only heard. I visited the Palais de Versailles. "Now I know why the French Revolution happened," I wrote home on a post card. But I appreciated its beauty none-the-less.

After a week's stay there came to an end I wondered why the particular chord in me which would have made me sensitive to "mystique" of Paris, had remained untouched. So many of the devotees of this undeniably beautiful city attribute a magic to its charms, of which I remained unaware. Perhaps I had expected even more. I also think that in my first real encounter with western society I found, what I can only call the "commercialization of sex" rather repugnant; the very air seemed heavy with sensuality, so that even whilst enjoying myself, the puritan in my make-up recoiled from the physical expression of sex, going on all around me. Yet in spite of all these new and overwhelming experiences I was surprised to find that I was still the same person with the same dreams and desires, the same defects and anxieties. Europe had not yet succeeded in changing my essential self; I had expected a volcanic upheaval but there was only a disturbance on the surface. So still intact, mentally and physically, I left Paris for London where I was to spend the next three years; exciting stimulating years which enormously increased my knowledge of people, places and things; years of great happiness, so great in fact, that when at last I returned, I felt I was making a great sacrifice for India.

I could not have chosen a more interesting year than 1956

to be in England. Two outstanding events, the Hungarian Revolution and the Suez "fiasco", took place soon after my arrival in Europe and the full impact of these events was fully felt in London.

With the events in Hungary, the Iron Curtain was flung aside and it was clear that a radical change was taking place in the situation in Eastern Europe. I went to the Albert Hall where a great all-party rally was held in support of the Hungarians' right to freedom. I remember Jenny Lee remarking significantly that the Hungarian Revolution had proved that after all we were not nearing the state of affairs described in Orwell's "1984"; for it was the young people, trained and brought up under communism who were in the forefront of the struggle. Having known nothing but communism, still they were not blinded and deafened by it. Many Hungarian refugees fled to England bringing with them stirring tales of a people's revolution in a communist country, which was a true manifestation of the wishes of the people and not, as the communists would have it, a capitalist incited counter-revolutionary fascist plot.

At the height of the Suez crisis a mammoth gathering was held in Trafalgar Square by the Labour Party, to protest against the aggression upon Egypt. After the speeches and resolutions were over a procession was formed to march to Whitehall. I joined it and we had not gone far when the mounted Police who had been in the background suddenly charged. I discovered later that a Cabinet Meeting had been in progress at No. 10 Downing Street and that it was for that reason the demonstration was not allowed to proceed,

But at the time I was surprised and shocked. I had always thought of England as the citadel of free speech but this was like a re-enactment of scenes in India before Independence.

Both the events in Hungary and Egypt triggered off a great intellectual ferment in Britain and I quickly found myself involved in the battle of words. In England, never since the early thirties, had there been such a widespread interest in political and international affairs. One of the active centres of dialectic where I went often was the Universities Left Review Club, where meetings were held at that time in the unlikely surroundings of a plushy glass and steel night club in Oxford Street. Their awareness of the necessity for drastic rethinking on the problems facing society in the modern world, the wide range of subjects discussed, I found fitted in well with my own attitude. Not that the ULR was nothing more than a convector of hot air; there was an immensely practical side to their activities; they were concerned with the growing racial tension in many parts of London and conducted surveys into the social conditions in which the immigrant peoples were living; subsidiary groups concerned themselves with other educational and social problems. Many of the members were militant organisers of the Campaign for Nuclear Disarmament, often serving long terms in prison for their convictions.

I also joined the more sober Fabian Society and attended their meetings and week-end schools. Never before had I experienced the stimulation of intellectual companionship with so large and a varied number of people. Neither was this new awareness confined to politics. I had arrived just in time to feel the full impact of the new wave in the arts, which began with John Osborne's play "Look Back In Anger." He was among the first of the "angry young men" and was quickly followed by a number of others, novelists, playwrights, kitchen-sink-artists, Alan Sillitoe, John Wain, Kingsley Amis, Shelagh Delaney, all uniting in clamourous outcries against the Establishment : speaking eloquently for a section of people who had previously had no spokesman, making articulate the factory worker, the negro, the homosexual, the prostitute. In 1957 and 1958 "Declaration" and "Conviction" were published—the restatements of values, mainly of the younger generation of writers.

1958 saw the formation of one of the most dynamic political movements of modern times in Britain : the Campaign for Nuclear Disarmament, which achieved what the conventional political parties had failed to do—to arouse the enthusiasm and harness the energies of the young people of the country for a political cause. So powerful was its impact that similar organisations were formed in many countries of Europe in the next few years.

The inaugural meeting was held in the massive Westminister Hall in the heart of London. It was impossible to accommodate the thousands who joined the endless winding queues and an overflow meeting was held in an adjoining building. The platform was lit by a positive galaxy of "Stars." Bertrand Russell presided and among the speakers were J. B. Priestly, Michael Foot, Canon Collins and A. J. P. Taylor. I have attended hundreds of political meetings in my life but this surpassed them all in content and emotional appeal. Although I found a number of flaws in the arguments of C. N. D., I felt strongly that to sit back and allow the leaders of the nuclear powers to play with the destiny of mankind and threaten the whole future of civilisation was unpardonable and that the common man must have some means of voicing his objection to being a pawn in the political game and C.N.D. provided this. So I joined the marches to Aldermaston to express my solidarity with those who were working for peace. In that first march and the ensuing ones in which I took part I found the movement to be a meeting point for some of the most socially conscious and disinterested people I have met. True, like any mass movement it had its lunatic fringe, it embraced many widely differing points of view, from the communist to the Quaker. The majority, however, were Socialists—sincere, peace-loving people. I shall never forget the superlative organisation which arranged to sleep and feed thousands of marchers on a four day, fifty mile march, without leaving behind a scrap of litter behind.

London I found a wonderful place to live. There were countless opportunities for the pursuit of any interest—from dog-racing to the study of philosophy, from strip tease clubs to the practice of yoga. Just keeping one's eyes and ears open was an education in itself. I visited museums and art galleries, theatres and cinemas, concerts and ballets; attended lectures and evening classes; made new friends, men and women, and made love. I could return to my room high up in a tall building near the British Museum; I could close the door and there was complete privacy. Nobody interfered with my life; nobody offered me advice; nobody worried about me; nobody asked me awkward questions. I had never felt so free in my life. I worked and earned a sufficient amount of money. I was never seriously ill. Life was full and complete. I saved money to travel to Europe, to many countries and still newer experiences.

First to Germany. Travelling through this country eleven years after the end of the war I was able to realise in part what war had meant to Europe. But not until I arrived in Berlin and saw vast areas where nothing remained but dust and rubble was I able to grasp the fact emotionally. It was in Berlin too that I was able for the first time to witness communism in practice.

One clear Sunday morning I took the underground train from Kurfustendamm to Stalinallee in East Berlin. At the border station most of the passengers left the train. We waited there some time listening to repeated announcements warning us that the train was now leaving the Western Sector and would be entering the Russian Sector. At last there was a jerk and with a clanking of wheels my journey towards communism began. I looked around. There were only a few passengers. They were all old and looked gloomy but my spirits remained high in spite of them.

Stalinallee, the show piece of East Berlin is a wide clean street, with gay beds of flowers. I craned my neck to see the cream-coloured multi-storeyed buildings on both sides of the road. In contrast to the roads of West Berlin, there were few cars and in the whole of Stalinallee I could find only one shop (a woman's dress shop) which could be compared with the shops of West Berlin. Stalin in black stone gazed unperturbably over the street which bore his name (now dutifully changed since the cult of personality became taboo). Behind this pleasant facade lay street after street of ruin and desolation.

During my seven days stay I divided my time almost equally between the two Sectors. Berlin is, I think, the most fascinating city in Europe today. Here two opposing social systems glared at each other with unrelenting ferocity. In 1956 during my first visit, there was no restriction on movement between the two sectors and it was possible to investigate conditions with a fair amount of ease.

I saw refugees pouring into West Berlin in their hundreds, and was present at a number of "screening" interviews carried out by the West Berlin authority. Curiously enough, all those I saw on this occasion belonged to the working class; a machinist, the wife of a policeman, a tailor and a peasant farmer. Since I too belonged at that time to a truncated province of pre-independence India, I could well understand the pangs of a divided country. I know that no one leaves his hearth and home unless compelled by impossible circumstances.

Later in an interview with the Secretary of the Press Association of East Germany I said, "I am a socialist and think that a socialist system in superior to a capitalist one. You call your system socialist and therefore you and I can agree that it should be superior to the capitalist system over the border. Why is it then that I can see hundreds voluntarily leaving, to live under an inferior social system. The refugees I have met are average working people yet have left everything they have in a people's democracy to go over to West Germany. Why?" He tried to avoid a direct answer by saying that it was a complicated matter which would take a long time to explain. Also he had another interview very soon so would I put some other question. I pressed him to try to give at least a brief answer, since this problem had vexed me more than any other since my arrival in Berlin. "Our policy is good", he said "but a section of the people do not appreciate what is being done for them. They fall easy victims to high pressure propaganda that life is better in the West." I did not find this answer a very satisfactory one. It was quite apparent from what I had seen in East Berlin that communism could not provide anything like the same standard of life as that achieved by the West. The contrast was all the more striking, since by making a few minute's journey in the underground train it was possible to see the concrete results of two different methods of organising society. When the War ended in 1945 both sectors stood in ruins and were faced with identical problems of reconstruction. In the following 11 years two different worlds emerged and it seemed to me that the communist world lost on all counts. It offered neither a comparable standard of living, freedom of speech and association, nor even, to my dismay, intellectual honesty. I tried asking myself the question : where, if I were asked to make the decision would I choose to live? This did not involve abstract theorising, a weighing of the respective merits of communism and bourgeois democracy. It was simply a matter of how I would like to live my day-to-day life. Being a democratic socialist I therefore had no special fondness for either system, but seven days in Berlin had given me a clear conviction of what my answer should be. I should opt for West Berlin every time. Under the communists I should be faced by two alternatives; the renunciation of my socialist beliefs or incarceration in a prison or a labour camp. With all its defects the capitalist system has nurtured thinkers like Marx and Engels who have drawn upon its intellectual wealth to compose a death sentence on capitalism. This at least is a very positive factor in its favour.

Six years later I returned to Berlin. The gates were closed. It was a walled city; an obscene construction of wire and concrete sliced it in half. As long as it remains, the wall will stand as a monument to the failure of communism. Yet still in spite of the armed guard placed at all strategic points and the evacuation of those whose homes actually touch the wall, East Berliners continued to risk everything, even life itself to escape; crawling through tunnels, leaping from high windows, swimming canals, shot at and often killed. While I was there Peter Fleitcher lay dying from gun shot wounds in the no man's land between the two sectors. He called for help but neither side dared to move for fear of sparking off a major crisis, and he died there. In West Berlin that evening a demonstration was called out in protest. In the wake of the column of marchers came hundreds of cars blowing their horns. It seemed that in this impotent howling I could hear the warning signal of future conflict.

"To go away to Moscow; to drop everything here and go to Moscow." Like the three sisters in Tchekov's play I had often dreamed of visiting this city which is the centre of the greatest experiment in the organisation of society which the modern world has seen. In 1957 the World Festival of Youth was held there and I decided to go. I suppose that if I had travelled to Moscow straight from India I should have been impressed by its material achievements. But I was starting from London and as we proceeded through the spick and span neatness of Holland and on through Germany into Poland, the gradual deterioration in living standards was obvious. There seemed to be some improvement in the Soviet Union but even here the villages had a down at heel, neglected appearance.

Moscow itself is a big, bustling city with sumptuous underground stations and the magnificent Gorky Park of Culture and Rest where after an afternoon of sun and conversation I found myself on the verge of falling in love with Tamara, a beautiful Russian girl I had met. A member of the Young Communist League, she was sensitive, full of intelligence, honesty and gentleness. We arrived at that swift intimacy which is sometimes achieved by strangers on holiday and when I left at the end of the festival, she cried.

At that time economists were prophesying that the Soviet Union would not attain a comparable standard of living with Western Europe until 1970 and from what I was seeing all around me, I could not help thinking that there was a good deal of truth in their forecasts. Having already seen how Dutch peasants and Swedish workers lived, Russia seemed to be very far from being the Utopia that communists in other parts of the world imagined it to be.

Neither did there appear to be any more equality there than in the capitalistic West. There were disparities both in living conditions and incomes. While visiting a flat belonging to a Russian friend I came across some of the worst slums I had seen in Europe. Yet others obviously lived well and the "new class" were evident in the more expensive restaurants.

None of the officials or elderly people with whom I talked had any capacity to think for themselves. Discussions on politics, economics, art and literature quickly reached stalemate as the stereotyped doctrinaire formulae were trotted out. It was not possible to break through this defence mechanism with any appeal to reason or fact. I found the younger people delightful, openminded and prepared to concede a point if they could not defend it. I had no doubt that a future Soviet State in their hands would be much saner and more humane place than it is today. In many of the Russians I met I found a wonderful combination of warm peasant simplicity and urbane intellectual sophistication, which I did not find in any of the other industrial countries of Western Europe.

I was struck too by the absence of a public parade of sex which is so obvious in Western Europe. Here however they seemed to go to the opposite extreme and the atmosphere was quite Victorian. I saw no public demonstration of affection all the time I was there and I was told that even for a husband to embrace his wife on a railway station was frowned upon. It seemed a pity that some happy balance could not be arrived at, a compromise between Hyde Park on Saturday and the stiff formalism of Muscovite lovers.

My visit to Moscow took place four years after the death of Stalin and the destalinisation process was already one year old. Even so I had an experience which impressed upon me the terror which the Secret Police could instill in the minds of the ordinary citizens. I met a Russian girl, a student of psychology, who had expressed a wish to hear about yoga. We arranged to meet at my hotel but since I was engaged when she arrived, I asked her to wait for a short time in the lounge. When I returned to look for her she had disappeared. Much mystified I went in search of her and eventually saw her through the glass window of the hotel control office where she was apparently being questioned. After a few moments she came running out through the foyer into the street. I followed her, caught her up and asked her what was the matter. She turned, gave me a horrified look but would say nothing. I thought under the circumstances it would be better for her to go but then quite suddenly her mood changed, she became almost defiant, refusing to leave. I still remember her expression of terror, finding it more eloquent than all the books I had read about the horrors of the Stalin period.

One further curious incident happened to me while I was staying in this same hotel. One morning when I looked around for my camera before setting out for the day, I could not find it anywhere. I searched the hotel thoroughly but it was not to be found. I gave it up thinking that I must have left it outside during one of my sight seeing tours. The following evening it was back in my room reappearing as mysteriously as it had disappeared.

One of the most startling features of the Soviet Union, particularly, for one coming from a conutry with 76% illiteracy is the tremendous impact which education has had on the masses. On the underground, in the trams, people are reading; books of all kinds from technical volumes to poetry. I was asked by working people about such subjects as Ramakrishna, the 19th Indian mystic. In spite of the severe regimentation of the educational system and cultural life in general, there is a great enthusiasm for education, but the needs of a growing industrialised society, combined with a desire to maintain the continuity of the Russian cultural traditions have created contradictions which even the most heavy handed regimentation has been unable to iron out. In recent years too, the influx of foreign intellectual influences has added to the confusion, while the official line oscillates between the opposite poles of revisionism and dogmatism. There is no doubt however that the vast educational system that the communists have built up will ultimately lead to the dissolution of totalitarianism there. Knowledge is a two-edged weapon; it can be bent and twisted but it can also cut through restricting bonds to freedom.

With its common ownership, socialist-orientated education and the widespread dissatisfaction with the existing set up, I think that the Soviet Union is one of the countries where there are great possibilities for a real socialist advance in the coming years. So far the opposition has come mainly from middle classes and intellectuals but no fundamental change in the system is likely until the struggle percolates downward to the mass of working class citizens. There is no doubt that demands for a greater equality and more democratic functioning will be focal points in the conflict.

In this great land mass, a gigantic industrial complex has been built up at a fantastic rate, at the expense of much human misery and sacrifice, but as yet there has been little attempt to grapple with the enormous problems arising from the consequential growth, in any open-minded manner. Any attempt to do so would entail deviation from the rigid traditions of Marxism-Leninism. On the whole my reactions to the situation in Moscow are aptly summed up in the classic phrase of John Strachey: "The means have been terrible; the result commonplace."

On my return journey to London I stayed over for a few days in Warsaw. After the "Polish October Revolution" in 1956, it was at that time intellectually one of the most vital and stimulating places in Europe. A strong Western influence was clearly manifest in the realms of art, music, dress and the art of film. Nowhere had I heard so much vehement criticism of the Soviet Union. In fact towards the end of my stay it began to pall somewhat; it seemed to be marked by an excess of emotion and irritability. Yet it was in a way understandable. Surrounded by Germans and Russians, whom they hate and fear, they are in a helpless position. By temperament they are not inclined to accept their fate with equanimity. The scars of the last war remain, both on the city and in their minds; but what alternative have they but to lie low, sandwiched as they are between the two most powerful nations in Europe today?

Of all the communist countries I visited, Yugoslavia, I think, is the most exciting in its achievements. I have been there twice, in 1959 and 1963. One feels a real pioneering spirit there and some of the liveliest Marxist intellectuals I have ever met were Yugoslavs. Their experience with workers' self management, their efforts to decentralise political and economic administration, while maintaining the national unity of diverse peoples and the combination they have devised of common ownership with free market mechanism, are of direct relevance to many countries, whether communist or not.

There is also a considerable amount of cultural freedom. Of course, the system is still authoritarian and the grip of the Communist League, though somewhat relaxed, is still firm. Milovan Djilas' plea for the multiplicity of parties is still a voice crying in the wilderness but I have no doubt that the whole economic, political and social momentum in Yugoslavia, whether the Government likes it or not, is irresistibly pushing the country in that direction. In the meantime she has set the pattern which the whole of Eastern Europe is likely to follow in the coming years, though the pace of such developments will naturally depend on the relaxation of tension in Europe as a whole.

In Europe it was in the Scandinavian countries, particularly, Norway, Denmark and Sweden, where I found societies which most closely approximated with my ideals. The Labour parties have been in power there for long periods and have gradually brought about a more equitable distribution of wealth. Highly organised social security systems have been established and there is full employment, and all this with no loss of democratic freedom. Powerful co-operative and Trade Union movements have increased their influence both politically and economically, but although these are trends in the right direction, real socialism is still a dream of the future. Sweden has the highest standard of living in Europe. None of these countries can be accused of originally enriching themselves with colonial super-profits. However, large scale capitalism still continues to function everywhere, and wields powerful influence in spite of being "controlled". Nevertheless the working class is a potent factor in these societies, and is consciously bringing about quantitative changes through the Governments. So there is every chance that at a later stage there will be qualitative leap into socialism.

The longest period of my stay in Europe I spent in England and had good opportunities of studying the situation there closely. After the semi-revolution brought about by the Labour Government in 1945-51 many contradictions existed in the whole set-up. Large segments of the economy had been brought under public control but were being run in a totally bureaucratic fashion. When I questioned Hugh Gaitskell about this, asking if he did not think it incongruous from a socialist point of view, he replied "What can we do? The Trade Unions are not interested in greater responsibilities."

In the period from 1951—1964 the Conservatives held unbroken power and had set up the machinery which influenced the pattern of the whole social fabric. I realised how correct was the Marxian analysis which indicated the subtle ways in which the ruling class maintains its hold on a country. Its tentacles reach out in all directions—the church, the House of Lords, Royalty, the Public Schools, the press and mass media and even indirectly into the State system of education. For example, in a class in Philosophy which I attended, the Professor was sincerely expressing the view that if the Labour Party had its way Britain would soon have to submit to secret police and forced labour camps. When I challenged such an absurd statement, he quickly changed the subject. I must add, however, that I have attended lectures where the speakers did not conceal their socialist sympathies and there is of course full academic freedom and progressive thinkers are steadily increasing their influence.

One or two minor incidents which occurred while I was in England illustrate the somewhat curious parallelism which exists there. Situations persist when all things considered, they should cancel each other out. For instance, taking into account the prevalence of individualistic, capitalistic ethics for so long in the country, I thought it interesting that of all the countries in Europe, including the communist ones, I never saw more respect given to the pedestrian by the motorist. I have seen many people who consider themselves socialists, who, as soon as they get behind a steering wheel think that they are the lords of the road and that pedestrians are an inferior race. The fact that in addition to Britain's having been an imperialist nation, she has a long history of democratic struggle at home, has resulted in this civic virtue.

On another occasion I was able to get an idea of the impartial working of the British judiciary. An Indian sailor was alleged to have murdered two of his mates on the high seas between Liverpool and New York and was brought to England for trial. I acted as his interpreter in both the lower and the higher Court. Now, here was a foreigner, who had allegedly committed the most heinous of crimes, yet he was provided free of cost with a lawyer, who was a Queen's Counsel, to defend him. As I sat in the court looking at the judge and the jury, the prosecution and defence counsels, the police, the gaolers and lesser clerks of the court I used to wonder how much the whole proceedings was costing the British tax-payer. As for myself, I have never been paid more for a short-term job. I tried hard to discover defects in "bourgeois" system of justice but failed. Every possible precaution was taken to see that there was no miscarriage of justice and ultimately the man was acquitted. Thus I was able to see a process which continued without a break, whatever Government might be in power. However much I disliked the Tories, I had to admit this much myself and I was led to the conclusion that no system whether communist or capitalist, can be condemned as a whole. There exist within a society, separate components, each with its own autonomy, history and aspirations; the lawyers, the doctors, scientists, engineers, artists and writers. No single key will unlock all doors and there is no black and white formula by which praise or blame can be allotted. Although there was nothing original in this observation it seemed to me to be of great value in these days of bitter ideological warfare, when things tend to get oversimplified in order to evoke popular emotion.

In 1958 I left for the Continent again to visit Brussels to see the Universal Exhibition. Since I had already seen the city on a previous occasion, I felt that I could devote all my time to the exhibition itself. I used to spend every day there from 10.0' clock in the morning till 7 at night, but even after seven days I still did not feel that I had really covered everything to my satisfaction. I found it a tremendously exciting experience; the immense variety in human creativeness was breath-taking. Wandering along the flower bedecked paths, by fountains which played at night in a mist of changing colours and still pools where flamingoes cast their rose pink reflections among the water lilies, passing from one pavilion to another, I was amazed at the astounding diversity of man's needs and his even more diverse and ingenious ways of fulfilling them. Here was the world in miniature indicating the limitless fields of human inventiveness.

Dominating the Exhibition in size were the two massive pavilions of the U.S.A. and the U.S.S.R., both challenging expressions of their specific cultures. If only they could co-operate instead of trying to destroy each other, what a difference it would make to the world. Beneath all the gloss and glare of affluence lay the seeds of total destruction and as I admired the technical and artistic skill of the many different nations displayed there, I could not help remembering that at the press of a switch, everything that through the centuries man had built up could be reduced to heap of radio-active ash.

Although I visited a number of countries in Europe, and tried to study some special aspects of each country which seemed important to me, what I was ultimately interested in was the total impact of the industrial civilisation of Europe, both in its western and eastern manifestations and its moral and spiritual significance.

To someone arriving from India in Europe, the first difference of which one is made aware is in the realm of human relationships. A group of us who had travelled together on the boat had arranged to meet again in London a month after arrival to compare notes. All of them were impressed with the same factor. One, a half-baked Marxist, with a flair for stereotyped phrases said, "it is all cash-nexus". I disagreed. Selfishness and greed exist everywhere, so do human sympathy and love. Any such broad generalisation would at the best be a half truth. Yet there certainly was a difference. There was much less self-conscious shyness, which is so apparent, particularly among young people in my country, and human contacts were much more open, easy and expressive. It was not necessary to obtain a formal introduction before starting a conversation with a girl one did not know. There was much evidence of self-sufficiency, particularly among, the girls, which generated a feeling of independence, and which I liked very much. In India most relationships are bogged down by extra-personal factors; the family, caste, custom, tradition, public opinion; all combine to impose a a certain artificiality and self-consciousness which considerably restrict freedom of expression.

It is true that often the opportunities available in Europe are misused, in that independence is frequently not sustained by clear thinking, uncontaminated by all the pressures of mass communication. After a few weeks one might easily come to believe that somehow one's capacity to receive love is tied up with the tooth paste, soap or cigarettes one uses.

Also with the development of this sense of autonomy and individuality, relationships have become more conscious and lost some of their spontaneity. Everything is so clearly defined that there is much less scope for any romanticism. Let me illustrate what I mean. I was once asked by an Italian motorist, who was giving me a lift, whether I had visited Naples. When I said I had not, he exclaimed "Oh, then you have not seen the real Italy". I asked him to explain. "In the North there are many factories; people are always looking at their watches. They have no time to live. In Central Italy there is too much Catholicism which kills all spontaneity. But in Napoli it is different. There, two and two might be six or five, or a rose or love—or anything. In Milan it is always four". Obviously he thought that something valuable had been lost; that volcanic surge of feeling which carries all before it, counting no cost. Very often I think the mental and emotional capacities and attitudes in pre-industrial societies have a tendency towards this kind of exuberant and impulsive expression; they have not been torn by scepticism and are still able to react passionately to ideas and symbols.

Born and brought up in a society with a strict and rigid social structure, I myself would find it difficult to lose myself with such instinctive abandon, but I also feel that in Northern

Europe a little more romanticism mixed with the highly rational, even calculating disposition one finds, would not be amiss. While I was living there I came closer to understanding the conflicts between the austere disciplined classicism and the bursting emotional brilliance of romantic expression and was able better to appreciate the impassioned complaints of a writer like D. H. Lawrence that the European had "sex in the head" and was losing his capacity for direct and simple feeling.

Here again I feel that it should be possible to arrive at a synthesis. However much I disliked what seemed to me the almost mercenary consideration which concerned people in their relations with others, I also recoiled from the uninhibited expression of the Italians with their loud argumentation, brawling and unashamed chasing of foreign women. "No woman is unhappy when asked to make love," they would say and acted accordingly. However, such a balance cannot be organised by society. It is something which each individual must attain for himself, although to some extent educational and social training can help in the process.

I have mentioned earlier that among the Muscovites I found a large measure of naturalness, perhaps because many of those with whom I came into contact were families which had been peasants a generation or two ago. In one of a number of interesting exchanges I had with a crowd outside the Kremlin I was asked what I liked most about the Russians. I said that I was most impressed with their basic simplicity. A quite smartly dressed girl in the group seemed annoyed and asked sharply, "Do you think we are primitives?" "Certainly not!" I replied, "but even so, do you not think that it might be a good thing if we were able to retain some of the good qualities of the primitives?" She did not seem at all convinced and turned away indignantly.

Later I gathered in England that if you said that a person was simple it implied that he was not quite "all there". The popular belief was that only fools were simple; intelligent people were complicated. "What a complex personality he is", is considered to be a compliment, even if that complexity is giving an immense amount of trouble and even leading to mental instability. Yet it seems to me that a really intelligent person should be able to preserve an integral simplicity and while being aware of secondary facts, should not be distracted by them from the fundamental truths which govern our lives.

The age of innocence, however, has gone for ever, even for we Indians. Any attempt to maintain simplicity at a primitive level is impossible in our modern civilisation. At the same time it is evident that the turmoil of present day existence is bringing about a state of serious mental and spiritual malaise. Is this an inevitable and unavoidable development? My four years in Europe convinced me that it need not necessarily be so. I met a large number of people, who, while being sensitive and open to every form of influence, managed, in spite of it to keep a still centre at the core of their personalities.

Also my brief experience of the Chinese culture and civilisation in Hongkong and Taiwan convinced me that society can be built up on the basis of secular ethics. The main difficulty in Europe to my mind is that for hundreds of years the whole structure was based on God-centred ethics. Therefore, when the conviction that "God is dead" became prevalent it brought in its wake a profound moral and spiritual crisis. We are seeing the beginnings of the same problem in our own country at the present time. Of course the fundamental change in outlook which is required is not at all easy and the period of transition is likely to be a very difficult one.

We hear a great deal these days about "the end of ideology". In a way it is true that the unevenness of human knowledge, and the contradictory philosophical implications of the different intellectual disciplines cannot provide us with the *weltangschauung* of the nineteenth century, which started with a scheme of the universe and then drew its human implications. It is no wonder that Kierkegaardian revolt against Hegelian abstraction has assumed tremendous proportions. Any system, today, has, in order to be meaningful to start with the human conditions, since in that at least, there is no ambiguity.

In the modern industrial society witnessed in Europe, the impersonality of the system, its emphasis on mathematical accuracy, the continuous efforts to improve material conditions, tend to make individuals "outer-directed", depriving them of the ability to develop an inner richness and bringing about the state of alienation described so aptly in David Reisman's "The Lonely Crowd". Yet I am convinced that this need not necessarily be the outcome of industrialisation. The advanced societies of Europe are able to provide such wonderful opportunities for all sections of the people to develop themselves in every possible way. The old class divisions and barriers are rapidly disintegrating, and the conception of an ideal society in which all are free and equal, is no longer a Utopian dream. Now conscious efforts have to be made to reduce the wear and tear of living in the modern world. Speed, noise, the blazing intrusions of mass media on the human mind, all combine to blind the sensibilities, to make man subject to all kinds of tensions and psychological disorders. Some headway can be made in the solving of this problem by the reduction of working hours, the cultivation of leisure and the development of deep inner awareness, of ourselves and the world around us. But an intellectual discipline while starting from the individual should then reach out into a wider social reality. It is possible to evolve in this way, a broad social philosophy which would be acceptable to all men, in whatever ideology they may believe. In the struggle between capitalism and communism, it is increasingly being realised that the advanced industrial societies are facing a number of problems, whichever system is being followed, and the solution to these problems cannot be so very different either. In fact, the present ideological cleavage is rather a continuation of the momentum of the past, than a result of the existing differences. In getting to know both Eastern and Western Europe, I discovered that the same underlying human realities and aspirations govern the actions of all men. It is feasible that atheists, agnostics, believers, in all nations could all subscribe to a common, social philosophy which expounds the combination of individual happiness with social good, which takes into account the irrational element in man's make-up and transforms it into rational action.

My stay in Europe cured me of a number of illusions. The first was the assumption that greater economic development or material advancement automatically bring about moral and intellectual progress. An Indian journalist writing about his impressions of Britain after six months stay there, said he was surprised to find that most people were more interested in football pools than the arguments about nuclear war. He had obviously thought that in the affluent society there would be a greater degree of intellectual awareness and social consciousness. There is not. The improvement of economic conditions may stop the tendency to cheat the bus conductor or to steal milk bottles from door steps but it does not impel individuals to attain true moral heights. Similarly it is one thing to provide cultural amenities for the people, but quite another, to guarantee that they are used properly. I used to see this after the office rush hour in the Westminister Public Library in London, where thousands of books on every conceivable subject, from westerns to abstract philosophy and scientific tracts lined the cases. It goes without saying that the majority went for the thrillers, detective stories, westerns, romances, light escapist fiction of every kind. Is it possible to change such a state of affairs ? Is it desirable ? To feed minds rather than condemn them to a perpetual diet of candy floss. There are only two ways; by only supplying books which are desirable or by a long and arduous process of education in discerning what is really "valuable". The first method is one of dictatorship, the way of book burning and suppression, of rigorous censorship. The second is the only way for a free country, but it will need not only education in the right use of amenities but education of a far subtler and more complex kind, entailing the development of the whole man.

My second illusion concerned the working class. Coming from a country where physical labour was despised I had nevertheless always believed in the dignity of manual work. During my stay in England I did a variety of jobs involving physical work, in restaurants, the post office, clubs and hospitals. None of it particularly strenuous but it brought me into close touch with the British working class, the 'oldest working class' in the world and one which certainly cannot be termed the "lumpen Proletariat", since it is a vital force in the British Labour movement. I visited the houses of the working people, attended social occasions, such as dances and socials and became friendly with a number of them, both men and women. Nowhere, however, did I find any one who seemed bestowed with divine powers which will alter the whole course of history. They were actually human beings like every one else, with the same strength and frailties. Since the war a greater social mobility has developed with the extension of further education and general improvements in the material environment of working people. Young people are no longer destined to remain for ever the same 'class' as their parents and I was impressed with the number of self-educated working men whom I met. But I did not feel that I should have to *declasse* myself in any way in order to identify myself with the working class and the socialist movement. In fact, I had the impression that in Britain a large section of the working class was no longer regarding itself as such and if questioned would assess themselves as middle class. Middle class snobbery, I regard with contempt, but many socialists, seem to think it necessary to create an artificial working class snobbery. It seems to me that the allegiance to universal human values and the efforts to put them into practice should forge a common bond between all "classes". However, the rich tradition of solidarity in the working class movement should not be allowed to dissipate with the improvement in the conditions of working people.

The two things I liked most in Europe, were the countryside and European women.

In Western villages one can find the peace and freshness of the country without being deprived of all the amenities of modern civilisation. Radio, television, newspapers and the post office keep you in touch with the outside world, and it was in the village that I found the balance I was seeking between industrial and agrarian societies.

One of the features I dislike about India is the position of women in society; dominated by their husbands and relations, almost their entire existence is confined within the house. Even among the educated the superficial modernism and sophistication is often found to be only a veneer. Scratch a little bit and underneath you find the traditional women, with the same reactions as their less advanced sisters, often torn by so much conflict that they find it difficult to face any real challenges effectively. I am not blaming Indian women. Often these days one finds as much indecision and ineffectiveness among the men. Perhaps at the present stage in our development it is the inevitable reaction to the changing society in which we are living. Now in Europe I found a large number of different kind of women—emancipated from the heavy burden of the bondage of the past, genuinely interested in a wider range of experience outside the home and family, without losing their essential femininity. I liked it very much, and have no doubt that in the course of time more and more of our own women will develop in this way, following the examples of many famous Indian women who have distinguished themselves in many spheres of life.

My visit to Europe gave a sense of perspective with which I could view my own country. Many of the good and bad things which are happening in European society will soon be happening in India. Therefore, my criticism of the European situation does not contain any "nationalist" element. Most Indians, for example, are extremely critical of the high divorce rates in Europe, and feel superior that our own rate is lower. But I have no doubt that when we reach the same stage of industrial development we shall not be behaving very differently in this and other matters, unless we are forewarned and through social and educational policies manage to avoid the pitfalls in which others have been trapped. In fact, the single biggest challenge that we face in India today is how we can construct an industrial society, with as few of the detrimental effects of industrialization as possible, and in the process rid ourselves of many of the more irksome aspects of Indian society. In this, we are fortunate, in that we have the experience of the West on which we can draw to our advantage.

My visit to Europe strengthened my belief in modernism without overlooking the attendant problems, yet, when I calculated the pros and cons of an industrial society I found the positive advantages far greater than the disadvantages.

In fact when I returned to India, and looked around with the added experience of Europe I could not help asking myself in what way I could say that contemporary Indian society was superior to that of Western Europe—economically? culturally? educationally? politically? socially? morally? spiritually? To my consternation I could find none. I asked others the same question, particularly those who considered India to be a wonderful country. All expressed deep emotional attachment but apart from two points, they were unable to make any categorical statement of superior values. These two points I find interesting. The first one was that more satisfying and lasting human relationships were developed and the second, that religious awareness was more universal. Any perceptive observer of the Indian scene would testify that in both these aspects of life a deterioration has now set in. My own feeling is that perhaps in the realm of religion India still has something positive to contribute. In most other spheres we will have to learn from the west and apply the knowledge we gain in an imaginative and creative manner to our own special conditions.

CHAPTER V

"Culture is the passion for sweetness and light, and (what is more) the passion for making them prevail." — Matthew Arnold.

When I consider all the experiences, thoughts, feelings and memories which make up the fabric of life, I often ask myself : "How much Indian am I? What does being an *Indian* involve?"

As an Indian I have inherited much from my Indian tradition, but also during the formative years of life I lived under British rule. For anyone belonging to the educated middle class, living in a city, and having close relations who had direct experience of Europe, contact with certain amount of British cultural tradition was inevitable. However, the main influence during my youth was undoubtedly Indian rather than European.

Indian culture today is, however, in a stage of transition and as we move towards the twenty first century it seems to me that it is necessary to discover which aspects of Indian life are worth preserving and to be prepared to reject others, without being branded "un-Indian". Because of the immense complexities inherent in our changing society, this examination can be conducted on a personal basis : I can try to determine what I am and what I would like to be and thus project the macrocosmic view through the microscosmic.

Nevertheless when I indicate what I would like to be I do not intend to do so in exclusive personal terms, isolating myself from the cultural milieu by creating a private world of meanings and symbols. It is not the individual pursuit of private desires but the achievement of certain desirable and attainable social goals which should be aimed at. We will have to work with all our strength and with all our faith towards change in ourselves, and thus bring about transformation in our society.

In what direction should this change take me? How can I be progressive in thought and action without losing touch with the broad mass of society, and what kind of India would I like to see evolve, of which I can feel myself a part?

Even when one has tried to define what one is, and what

one wants to be, the description is still far from complete. The continuous and delicate tension between these two states of being, manifest in the thought and behaviour of the individual is a factor which is never constant. I am no longer at forty-three what I was at fourteen. My physical body has been completely renewed several times, and yet beneath all the change, that strange phenomenon, memory, integrates the personality, preserving continuity. To be able to apprehend this elusive essence in men's nature which fluctuates between actuality and aspiration is to understand what culture is. It can be caught fragmentarily in art and literature, more effectively perhaps than by analysis. Being neither an artist nor a poet I can only try to analyse and define the nature of this evanescent substance we call culture, and Indian culture in particular.

What is the nature of this India I have inherited? About 530 million people inhabit the Indian Union. They speak seventeen recognised languages with sixteen different scripts. Of these I can understand only five, read three and speak two. In addition there are over eight hundred dialects. There are seven religions, six different ethnic groups, innumerable castes and sub-castes among the Hindus. As in other countries there are also stratifications of classes. In this fascinating mosaic I am only one small fragment. Is there anything specifically *Indian* about me, or any other inhabitant in this vast sub-continent? A man living one thousand miles away in the South may differ from me in practically every aspect, ethnic religious, caste, language, eating habits and dress. I cannot even communicate with him unless he happens to know a foreign language or we have another Indian language in common. Can it be said that either of us is more typically "Indian"? Yet if I meet this Southern stranger in a foreign land, I have no doubt that he would call forth a response from me which no non-Indian would. True it is possible that after a very brief encounter I may develop a positive dislike for him as an individual, may henceforth avoid him like the plague, but how does this response occur in the first place? Is it because we share a common history and find a certain common denominator in the national unconscious? Or, is there a feeling that we shall have similar reactions to India's triumphs and tragedies? Is it that although my feelings for my country are purely subjective, rooted in personal associations, when I meet another Indian I am prone to generalize, attributing the same feelings to him also? I imagine that he must also nourish a secret longing for India's wide skies, her crowded and dirty streets, her beautiful hills and forests, that he must venerate her great saints and poets, her statesmen and revolutionaries simply because I do. Does India represent a mood, a philosophy, a way of life, to which all of us, whether we are conscious of it or not, and in spite of our differences, in same way owe allegiance?

Many would question the existence of common national feelings. Certainly it may be argued that twentyfour years ago our nationalism was sufficiently weak to allow the partition of India on the basis of religious sentiment. Today the existence of strong fissiparous tendencies in many areas, such as Nagaland and Kashmir, indicate that if it does exist it is not uniform throughout the country. However, when the country is faced by a threat from outside as in 1962 from China and in 1965 and 1971 from Pakistan, it is clear that whatever differences might exist, in a time of emergency all these are submerged and an overwhelming unity is forged.

On these occasions Indian "nationalism" was put to a severe test. Many acute foreign observers prophesied that India would be torn apart by communal violence during the first Indo-Pak conflict, but their gloom proved unjustified. That is why I for one have no undue worries about India's disintegration due to lack of "nationalism". The underlying unity of the Indian people is made of sterner stuff than most people would credit.

This is not of course to deny that the chauvinism of individual linguistic groups does not exist, but this hardly finds its expression outside the framework of Indian polity. The development of Dravida Munnetra Kazhagam (DMK) in Tamil Nadu, the most organised and articulated of the separatist groups, is an example. It began its existence with the slogan of "independence of South India from northern domination" but ended with the demand for greater autonomy for the State and equal status for all the Indian languages. Moreover, it is interesting that DMK's appeal, which is meant for the whole of South India, is largely confined only to the Tamil Nadu State. After forming the State Government in Tamil Nadu it seems DMK is well absorbed in the Indian political system.

This does not mean that India might not fall apart for other reasons. There are political factors : irreconcilable groups have gained control in certain areas and they might try to win over other parts of the country by civil war. This might mean temporary dismemberment of the country which might be given a long lease if foreign powers became involved. But this would not invalidate my thesis that there does exist a basic "oneness" in India. Long political separation, however, would tend to corrode this unity, since succeeding generations would grow up with different experiences and memories.

What is this 'Indianness' which brings Indians living widely apart together ? First, there is the acceptance of the outer formalities of living, the holding of the same passport, respecting the same Constitution, being subjected to the same economic policies, familiarity with the same code of law, voting in the same elections, etc. Once returning overland to India, I walked across the Franco-Swiss border near Geneva. Only a few yards of earth separated the two countries and the people living across the border could not have been so different. Yet one could clearly see the change, by the greater prosperity on the Swiss side of the border. Just as in partitioned Bengal it made the world of difference in the last twenty years on which side of the border one has been living.

Out of these collective experiences of common life there emerges a common memory. This is the ultimate factor prevailing in the sense of one-ness and unless a section of the country's population opposes any aspect of this memory, or feels alienated from it, then it tends to remain as a positive factor. But it is a passive element, only manifesting itself in combat, whether it be a test match in cricket or an international conflict.

..When we were students our history lessons dealt with the history of India, not just the history of Bengal. In fact, we read only the highlights of Bengal's history within the wider history of India. The history of India is the story of the continual rise and fall of empires, the constant efforts of one conqueror to bring the people under one rule. Lack of communication meant that control was inevitably rather loose, and none of these empires ever succeeded in occupying the whole area covered by the Indian Union today. In particular the South maintained its independence and a considerable degree of autonomy was also held in the Eastern States.

However, the spread of Hinduism, which penetrated the South and eventually found some of its most authentic expression there, compensated for this lack of political consolidation. Sanskrit was the link language but it was a language for the elite. For the illiterate population the mythology which developed around religion was a more potent factor and the places of Hindu pilgrimage extended from Rameswaram in the southernmost tip of India to the snow-bound Himalayas in the north. So in spite of its many diversities, India for the Hindus was one country. But what of Indians who do not share the Hindu religion and its mythology? Is India then a land of Hindus where others are "aliens"? Hinduism is a product of India but so are Buddhism, Jainism and Sikhism. Both Buddhism and Jainism are virtually integrated in Hinduism with their prophets having taken the place of *Avatars*. Sikhism is wholly rooted in the Indian sub-continent. Being a small community Sikhs are very conscious of their own identity. Although there have been attempts to promote distinct Sikh nationalism, it has not and is not likely to be disconnected from the main stream of Indian nationalism.

Zoroastrianism was brought to India by the persecuted Persians but it is not proselytising religion and remains confined to the Parsees, who also being a small minority community have zealously preserved their identity. Through the centuries however their links with Persia have been lost and they have been absorbed into the Indian community. Consequently it is not with these religious minorities where the main issue lies but with the much larger groups professing Christianity and Islam.

With the arrival of St. Thomas in the first century India was one of the earliest countries to receive Christianity. But the real impact of Christianity was felt only after the arrival of West Europeans on Indian soil. The South was the fertile ground, since it was here that the harsh rigidities of the Hindu caste system and the evils emanating from that system operated most strongly. Christian teachings were also welcomed by the depressed groups, particularly among the tribal peoples. Among

Indian Christians there are I think two main cultural groups — those who were converted from Hinduism, and those converted from animism.

I have lived in South India for nearly two years and had a number of friends there who were Christians. I found that in many instances Hindu customs and superstitions had permeated their Christianity. Some even married within their own caste! I also found that the Catholic Church had accepted many of the rituals and formalities of Hinduism. Jesuits with whom I have discussed the subject offer highly intellectual explanations regarding the compromise. But although Christians do consider themselves as a group apart from the Hindus, I never had the feeling that they were in any way separate or alienated from the Hindu society as a whole.

The position of Christians who were converted from animism is somewhat different. Through Christianity they came to know about the wider, modern and sophisticated world. They were completely overwhelmed by the intellectual superiority of Christianity. Their tribal beliefs, customs and memories did not have sufficient strength to withstand the pressure, especially in the case of the younger generation. The renunciation of tribalism created a spiritual vacuum which was almost entirely filled by the new religion. Therefore, their capacity for the absorption of Christianity was much greater than those who were converted from Hinduism. Consequently the gulf between the Christians converted from animism and from Hinduism was wider than between the Hindus and the converts from Hinduism.

It is also possible to differentiate between those Indian Christians who live in the central areas and those who inhabit the more outlying parts of the sub-continent. Christians living say in Bihar or Madhya Pradesh are so landlocked that they cannot help being influenced by their Hindu environment and Christian missionaries cannot prevent constant interaction between the two religious groups. Although they try to insist on their separate identity, slowly they become absorbed into the broad flow of Indian life.

This is not true of Christians in outlying areas like Assam. Not only are the people there physically more remote (except for a handful who go in for higher education) but there also is the counter-attraction of other neighbouring countries like

China and Burma and for some obscure reasons Western Christian missionaries seem to encourage separatist movements. For some time to come it seems as though this area will trouble India's rulers with the problem of national identity.

The history of Islam in India is more complicated. It was brought to India by Muslim conquerors and its methods of conversion have often been more aggressive than those of Christianity. Many characteristics of Hinduism must have been particularly repugnant to the followers of the Prophet. Islam has a specific edict against image-worship and the Hindus must have seemed incorrigible image-worshippers. Also the gross inequalities in the Hindu social structure combined with a tendency to treat outsiders ("mlechchhas") with contempt and to keep them outside the pale, were additional factors for regarding Hinduism with distaste.*

However, there have always been liberal Muslims. Akbar the Great was an outstanding Muslim who wanted to achieve a synthesis of all religions. The cult of Sufism influenced the most enlightened and sophisticated and created a philosophical bridge between Islam and Hinduism. The impact of Islam on Hinduism or vice versa on a religious plane has been negligible. Whereas the cultural influence of the Muslims in Indian life has been wide-ranging and profound especially in the realm of architecture, music and literature. Hindus cremate their dead, while Muslims bury them in a grave. Above such a grave rose Taj Mahal, one of the most beautiful monuments in the world, in which every Indian takes pride. Many Hindu poets and writers have been inspired by the love story of the Emperor Shahjehan and Mumtaz. Hindusthani classical music is mainly a Muslim contribution but it is a common heritage for all Indians, and Urdu with Arabic script is the common language of Hindus and Muslims in large areas of the country. Yet despite all these positive influences, there were many factors which brought about a widening of the rift between the two communities.

The Muslims form the largest single minority in India. Before the arrival of the British it was the Muslim rulers who dominated the northern part of the country and consequently after the advent of the British rule the leaders of the Muslim

* This section was written before the 1971 conflict and the emergence of Bangladesh.

community had the feeling that they had been ousted from their rightful place. Feelings of rancour led to a boycott of the British in the initial stage. This attitude was reversed by Sir Syed Ahmed and then there developed the fear that if the British withdrew, the majority of Hindus would deny them their legitimate place in Indian society. This was confirmed in 1937 when the Congress Party in the United Provinces, in spite of a previous agreement, barred the Muslim representatives from the Congress Cabinet and gave encouragement to the separatist movement of the Muslim League, which stood clearly for the partition of the country on a religious basis and the creation of the Muslim State of Pakistan. If the country had not been partitioned then the gradual absorption of Muslims in the Indian polity would have been possible.

The emergence of Pakistan has complicated the psychological outlook of the average Indian Muslim. The bitterness which was generated at the time of partition will not be easily forgotten and periodic outbursts of communal rioting in Pakistan and India have tended to upset any positive gains which might have been achieved. Many of those who were in the forefront of the struggle for Pakistan remained in India after the partition and tried to make the best of bad situation. Many grew disillusioned about the way the things developed in Pakistan at least before the emergence of Ayub Khan. In return for the security of their community they offered votes to the ruling Congress Party.

Among those less educated, religious feeling runs strongly and the appeal of Pakistan is irresistible but only a minority would risk giving active support to promote Pakistani interests.

Likewise there is a minority who would identify themselves wholly with India. It can be safely assumed that twenty-four years has not been a sufficiently long period to resolve the psychological complications of an average Indian Muslim in terms of Indian "Nationalism". Further complications have arisen since the Indo-Pak conflict in 1965. Although a number of Indian Muslims died fighting against Pakistan and there was no communal violence in the country, large scale arrests of Indian Muslims in strategic areas, many of whom must have been innocent, convinced the Muslim leaders that there are suspicions about their loyalty to India. This created much resentment. Part of this feeling was manifest in the 1967 election when a sizeable Muslim vote swung against Congress as a protest. It means that while a minority of Indian Muslims completely identify themselves with Indian nationalism, another minority identify themselves with Pakistan, and the attitude of a large majority is not clearly defined.

To sum up, the feeling of nationalism does I think exist in the country in spite of diversities of language, religion and various stages of economic development. It is also true that a section of the Muslim and Christian population does not feel wholly identified with India, thereby detracting to some extent from the unity of the whole sub-continent.

The concept of nationalism is itself a new phenomenon in world history. It has coincided with the development of capitalism and modernization and the necessity for a centralised authority vested in the government. The first real expression of this nationalism was seen during the British rule. Until then Indian nationalism was in existence in a historical and spiritual sense, but it was during the struggle against imperialism, (which itself brought about considerable unifying factors) that it developed to its fullest dimensions. Twenty four years after the attainment of independence, it still survives even after the severe tests in 1962 and 1965.

How then do I feel that I, as an Indian fit into this India? Do I feel landing in Bombay after a long period abroad that I am coming 'home'? Do I feel 'at home' in Kashmir or Kerala, nearly 1,500 miles away from Calcutta, which is where I live?

The last time I returned to India by boat, the sight of the distant coastline made me catch my breath with excitement and being in Bombay certainly had a qualitative difference from being in Brussels or Beirut. People looked more or less, as I did; I could understand what was being said around me; I could eat Indian food, even with a little effort, Bengali dishes. The papers were full of Indian news and over the radio came the strains of Hindi film songs. Everywhere was the familiar bustle, dirt and poverty.

Yet however evocative are the sights and sounds of Bombay, I do not belong there. It means another 1,200 miles journey across country, before the most intense feelings are aroused. Steaming into Howrah Station I am assailed by memories of boyhood days, where so often we greeted or bade farewell to relations and friends. Passing over the Howrah bridge, fanned by the cool breeze of the river Hooghly I draw closer to the heart of Calcutta. The broad green expanse of the maidan, with its herds of goats, the lanes and byways, the effervescent crowds, all movement and colour, are loaded with meaning for me. At last self and place are identified. As I have lived always in South Calcutta, it is that part of the city for which I feel greater attachment. Although I have stayed in a number of houses, when I visit Netaji Bhawan in Elgin Road I can once again relive my childhood days. But today it is not until I finally reach the flat where I now live with my wife that I can feel at last I am home. The journey from Bombay Port to Calcutta proceeds in gradations of intensity in the sense of belonging and reaches its climax in a flat in Jodhpur Park in South Calcutta.

My home is in West Bengal. My language is Bengali. I do not have to face the complications of those who were born and brought up in East Bengal and now have to live in West Bengal. I have inherited the Bengali cultural tradition which is quite distinct from cultures in other parts of the country. We have our own ways of cooking, dress, our own folk music, handicraft, rich literary tradition, our own art, film and drama. There are also certain trends in religious tradition associated with the cults of Kali and Vaishnavite philosophy, and in the political sphere Bengal has a reputation for "terrorism" and left politics.

The fact that I was a member of a middle class family in West Bengal has enabled me, through my education, to make this cultural tradition a part of my heritage, but has also in a sense created a gulf between myself and those with whom I want to communicate—the deprived people of India, who because of their poverty are denied access to these treasures.

All these factors, my being born as a Bengali, as a Hindu, as a Calcuttan, as a member of a family with a specific family background (fortunately caste is a negligible factor in urban Bengal) produce divisive factors in my Indianness. Nevertheless as I have suggested above, in the context of the all-India situation these disruptive agents do not altogether erase "Indianness" which is a habit, a warm comfortableness with the familiar, which most people accept without thinking. What does work against it, in my case, is my inability to accept anything without question. This always creates a gulf between me and my environment.

Moreover, I am never satisfied with things as they are. I want to seek out what is good and nourish it. To detect the worthless and reject it.

With the inception of British rule India's confrontation with the West began. The result was the cultural renaissance in the nineteenth century in which Bengal played a leading role. Faced with the influence of new ideas embodied in the Christian religion, liberalism and a scientific mode of thought, a number of notable religious reformers and artists emerged. The philosophical and religious response came from Raja Ram Mohun Ray, Keshub Chandra Sen, Ramakrishna Paramahansa, and Vivekananda and later Sri Aurobindo; the cultural synthesis came through Bankim Chandra Chatterjee and Rabindra Nath Tagore. The western world that preceded the first world war was a different world from that which rose from the ashes. It was then that the whole liberal world began to fall apart. Post-war frustration led to the growth of mass movements in many countries in direct opposition to liberal ideas. Communism and Fascism came into existence and prepared for another mammoth struggle. Freud plumbed new depths in the human psyche and brought an entirely novel approach to the study of psychology. T. S. Eliot wrote "The Waste Land".

The nineteenth century renaissance in Bengal touched only a small community of educated people. In the twentieth century the spread of education, the greater availability of newspapers, radio and cinema, had its impact on the masses and consequently, western influence has been much more widely felt and today the transistor has brought the outside world into the most far flung parts of India. As long as British rule continued there was a tendency, by a large and influential section of the people, to oppose the acceptance of foreign ideas. After the attainment of independence this restraint was slowly relaxed and gave way to a more balanced approach. This difference is apparent when we compare the attitudes that Gandhi had, with what his avowed followers actually do today.

The enormous programme of industrialization undertaken by independent India has been the other most powerful influence towards change in our country. During the British period communications had been developed and there were a few pockets of industrial growth which succeeded in affecting their surrounding areas. The three plans have considerably extended this pattern and have brought larger areas and more people into the vortex. Because of improved communications the effects are being felt further afield and there has been a marked increase in the capacity of the people to absorb new ideas. Already the social order is undergoing a transformation. The centuries old joint family system is breaking down; traditional religious beliefs and sentiments are being eroded. The symptoms of an industrialised society can already be discerned. The very basis of man's attitudes to his fellow men, to work and to the world in which he lives, is being undermined and new foundations are urgently needed.

Nineteenth century India faced conflicts of religion; the twentieth century faces the problem of religious scepticism. At one time the question was, how much modernism could be introduced into traditional life; now we face the problem as to how much traditional life may be allowed to continue, without affecting efficiency—the newly emerging god. These fundamental changes in the social matrix, call not for a cultural renaissance but for a veritable cultural revolution. I am using the phrase deliberately in spite of the disrepute into which it has been brought in Communist China. Revolution is necessary because of the wide range of changes needed and the rapidity with which these changes have to be brought about if we are to survive economically. Yet speed of action has to be combined with determined efforts to diminish the pangs of social change and to alleviate those feelings of alienation, which industrialization brings in its wake. Radicalism and realism have to be combined to achieve these ends.

The tensions and complexities of modern industrial societies, whether of the East or of the West, are such that new and unorthodox rather than traditional forms are required to give authentic expression to the frustrations, anguish and excitement of life in the atomic age. (Whether we are living in London or Calcutta, New Delhi or New York, we shall find increasingly more similarities than differences in our way of life). Yet in spite of its long history of industrialization differences among nations still persist in Europe. No one could mistake a Frenchman for a British, a German for a Russian. Each has his unique historic memory, speaks a different language, reacts according to his special "temperament." Even within the natural boundaries of these countries, local differences are perpetuated. Welsh and Scottish nationalists are strong enough to return M.P.s to Westminister. Foreigners in all places tend to band together and keep alive their own special cultures.

Living with an English wife frequently reveals the differences in attitudes between a developing and wholly industrialized society where each person is the part of a vast machine which exacts a strict conformity from each individual. Failure on the part of one, will affect the many. The passion for orderliness, discipline and punctuality are combined with the state of near collapse if anything goes wrong! Such discipline only comes slowly, creating its own frustrations and tensions which are the price every one has to pay for the good things which an industrial society provided. It is this stage of development towards which our country is advancing now and in the long run the only way of solving these problems is to reduce working hours so that the periods of stress and strain are less and more time is left for people to pursue their own interests. We shall also have to try and develop a "to be *and* not to be" outlook so that while absorbing ourselves completely in our work, we keep a part of the 'self' disinterested.

Increased industrialization affects the day to day life of the average man particularly the city dwellers, who are more susceptible to the incursions of western habits and customs. I remember when we were children we used to eat bread and butter for breakfast. This was considered by many of our friends and relations to be very western. But these days it is widely accepted in the towns and steadily spreading to the nearby villages as well. The reason is perhaps that it is easier to prepare such a breakfast than the more traditional varieties entailing sweating over a stove in the early morning. Now the time factor is increasingly becoming important. Scarcity of foodstuffs is also compelling Indians to change their food habits. Rice eating communities have been forced to eat wheat. Not only this, particular regional dishes are becoming familiar and even popular all over the country. Similarly certain items of European food are becoming quite common in big cities and are being consumed by those who are not western-oriented at all.

European dress, particularly among women, has not been adopted so quickly in this country, as in other Asian countries. For men, western dress is certainly more convenient for work in factories where the loose dhoti can be dangerous, but I cannot see why in offices western dress is necessary. There is, it seems to me, a hang over from the British Raj concerning the status symbol of western dress. Englishmen wore it and so did top Indian officials, but clerks and lesser officials wore Indian dress and so it came to be considered the dress of the 'babus'—the inferior breed. Somehow these ideas linger on. Otherwise who in their right mind would be seen walking about Calcutta in a temperature of over 100 degrees and 99% humidity wearing a suit complete with tie?

I was once talking to a group of young men who were quite westernized and were proud of it. It was a hot summer day; one and all were wearing terylene shirts. We were discussing western influences on India. I suggested that the most significant contribution made by western culture was her advocacy of rationalism and humanism. Now I asked, how could you rationally justify the wearing of terylene in our summer heat? They could not do so, but, terylene was "with it" so they wore it whether it made sense or not.

In fact, a superficial westernism often amounting to no more than unthinking snobbery, has become characteristic of a large section of the educated people, particularly, in northern and western India. This begins with the craze for English medium education. Not that I am opposed to English in principle; one foreign language should be taught in schools but the idea that unless one can speak English fluently one is not upto the mark is the sign of a slavish mentality and moreover leads to the neglect of the mother tongue. This blind imitation of all the least admirable features of western way of life shows a singular lack of creative imagination.

What do I as an Indian and a part of this society hope for, for our country? Can India remain long within the framework of her ancient ways? Is it even desirable that she should? I do not think so, neither do I think that modernism necessarily entails rootlessness. I do not reject some of the philosophical concepts of Hinduism, and there is much in our traditions, arts, crafts, music, from which I derive keen aesthetic pleasure. This appreciation is largely however a matter of familiarity. For centuries people have simply inherited religious beliefs and aesthetic preferences, and these were limited by family or at the widest point, national, culture. All systems of belief are ultimately shaped to suit the average man and in the past only exceptional people have felt the necessity to question the accepted creeds and customs and look elsewhere for solutions to the eternal questions of life and matter. As long as the world's culture developed more or less independently this presented no difficulties but now such isolation is disappearing. The idea of 'one world' is no longer a myth. A new age of inter-communication and interaction has dawned and mass media and education will tend to open up wider areas of cultural choice for the individual.

It is only when there are more people with open and adventurous minds that we shall be making the first tentative steps towards "one world". The physical steps are the simplest. Already the latest scientific and technological devices are being introduced into underdeveloped regions where the most primitive conditions prevail. Steel mills and skycrapers impose a drab uniformity upon the great cities of the world.

However, whatever changes may come within the social and economic structure, the cultural life of the people will still have to be based on the perennial values—the pursuit of truth, the cultivation of goodness and love, and the creation of beauty (Satyam, Sivam, Sundaram).

Is there a specifically Indian road in this pursuit of truth? Truth concerning objective existence; truth about man, society and universe? That two plus two makes four is true for the Chinese communist leader, the Indian peasant, the Russian engineer and the American businessman. How there can be a system of "Soviet Science", I have always failed to understand. It is true that Soviet scientists have made significant contributions to the common pool of human knowledge. How can it be theoretically different in nature from 'American bourgeois

Science'? Are Russian or American students taught different kinds of physics or chemistry or when Russian and American scientists meet do they speak in a way that is quite unintelligible to the other? Do the planes of Pan American and Aeroflot fly on the basis of different kinds of aero-dynamics?One can, of course, draw different philosophical implications—'idealistic', 'dialectical', or 'mechanical'—from certain scientific discoveries but this is in the realm of philosophy rather than science. There could also be a diversity of opinion relating to the use or misuse of scientific discoveries, but this entails the exercise of moral judgment and is not strictly a matter of scientific truth. Indians too may make outstanding contributions towards revelation of truth, but there can be no peculiarly Indian pursuit of truth. The first requirement in this search is the existence of academic freedom and the intellectual stimulus evoked by the inter-play of ideas from various schools is the best means of attaining the highest truth.

What about India's contribution to the cultivation of goodness? Although this century has witnessed some of the most extreme forms of barbarism imaginable, the struggle to establish the universal human values of freedom, equality and justice has continued unabated all over the world. Voices have been raised against colonial domination, racialism, exploitation of the weak by the strong, and man's inhumanity to man in prisons and forced labour camps. Here, India has a formidable task even within her own shores. The scourges of casteism and communalism have yet to be erased. To raise the poor and the oppressed to a reasonable standard of living is a task which will occupy all her ingenuity and energy for generations to come. Co-operation with those who face or who have overcome similar problems to ours will bring new vision and encouragement, and as we progress, support can be given to those struggling to establish themselves economically and socially in other parts of the world. Indian 'goodness' could ultimately find its highest expression in the pursuit of 'neighbourly love.'

In the realm of beauty India is able to give much from her ancient store of cultural treasures, to add to the richness of man's aesthetic response to the world around him. India is a land of many languages. Goethe said that learning a new language means gaining a new soul. Every language has its own peculiar atmosphere and embodies untranslatable words with their own particular nuances adding to our apprehension of reality.

India's classical cultural expression is deeply imbued with religious spirit. The concept of eternity is always in the background : there is a cyclic pattern in the nature of things. Unlike western ideas of progression which end in a climax, in India, man's endeavours might begin or end anywhere without being out of tune with nature. Even our music exemplifies our philosophy. Our songs do not end, they merely pause, leaving a lingering sweetness in the air.

Today how will a creative artist capture the mood and inspiration of modern India, conversant as he is with the style and the most subjective of all the arts has the greatest capacity to the most 'primitive.' The Indian composer familiar with Beethoven and Bach, Stravinsky and Schoonberg, has three paths open to him. He may remain a purist, working along traditional lines or he may break away from his inherited tradition and compose music in an entirely different tradition. Music being the most subjective of all the arts has the greatest capacity to withstand foreign influence but literature, painting and sculpture are more open to new trends.

How can an Indian painter be completely oblivious to all the developments in western art since the introduction of photography and the new scientific conception of reality? Can the logic of the abstractionists be waived on the basis of traditional aesthetics? I do think it is impossible for a creative artist in India to ignore these influences. Moreover, although the distinctiveness of India's culture will tend to decrease, at the same time the cultural influence of India will spread to other countries. This is already happening; a lively appreciation of Indian music and dance is developing in U.S.A., and other western countries while one has only to tune into any Indian Radio Station to find the influence of western music on modern Indian songs.

Will all the correlation of cultural patterns make the individual less Indian? I think it will. Will this mean that the creative artist is less authentic? This will very much depend on the individual. There are instances in the history of literature where a writer has become great although working on a foreign language. Ultimately it is a question of his capacity to synthesize within himself the diverse contradictory elements of reality and express his vision in a manner meaningful to others. The infiltration of external ideas naturally introduces complexities into the situation. The new vision can be richer, less insular, embodying the best of many cultures. Is the modern swinging Calcutta girl and her hipster sari, collecting Beatles records and queuing to see James Bond, very different from her contemporaries overseas ? Our students with their tight pants and pointed shoes are following similar interests and enthusiasms of students everywhere.

National boundaries are being broken down, international travel is on the increase, particularly among young people, where lack of money is no deterrent in these days of camping sites and youth hostels. All over the world one meets young men and women working their way across the continents, meeting people from other countries, seeing new and strange ways of life and many students find satisfaction in voluntary services in different parts of the world where their help is most needed.

Thus gradually the gulf between the nations is being bridged, by person to person relationships. We travel, learn languages, make friends. Politically we are beginning to realise that it is only by co-operation that small nations can meet the massive threat posed by the super powers. Yet there will remain the two biggest stumbling blocks to understanding : language and the existence of sovereign states. In the U.S.A. these have been largely overcome and she has been able to make relatively good progress. The same is true of the Soviet Union which is somewhat less homogenous, since unlike the U.S.A. it is not a new country. The Chinese colossus, with greater homogeneity, has begun to assert herself in Asia.

In contrast India is a sub-continent with much greater diversity and the democratic system tends to accentuate the differences. Today she has reached the point where she will have to strive towards greater unity or face disintegration. For twenty years we have had a centralized government — but after the fourth general election, when a number of States elected non-Congress governments the question of Central-State relationships became a question for serious discussion. The language question is another burning issue — setting the South against the North, Indian against Indian, trailing violence and death in its wake.

There has to be a link language, that is clear. It is a very delicate question but Hindi has ultimately to be adopted. The question is how soon the change can be peacefully effected.

I have asked myself why it is that I do not like flowery language, melodrama, ornate styles in furniture or architecture, all of which evoked admiration during other periods of history? Why is it that I prefer the plain statement, realist drama and simple, functional lines in modern design? It is, I think, a desire to reach the reality of things stripped of external decoration. The time has passed when life could be observed through the tinted glasses of religious, philosophical or political beliefs. The glass has been smashed. Facing reality is however a painful business. "Human kind can not bear too much reality", wrote T. S. Eliot. Most people at sometime or other seek escape and consolation in fantasy, religion, or a constant whirl of activity, but it is only when we are prepared to come to terms with reality to try to achieve truth in our relation with others — with the world around us that each man as himself and society composed of such men, will begin to move forward.

At the present time India is in a state of flux. The youth of our country are straining every muscle to be modern, yet self-consciously observing their own audacity, with one eye on the elders, who for their part are completely overwhelmed by the tidal waves of change sweeping across the land. Most innovations in any sphere of life are regarded with suspicion, whether they be of literary forms or fashion. The pattern of acceptance in relation to change is a fairly regular one. It begins with reactions of disbelief, disapproval, disgust or even horror and gradually diminishes as the new is absorbed or dies a natural death. The pendulum swings, skirts move from maxi to mini and back again, art from realism to surrealism. Like the Red Queen we run furiously after every new thing, only to find that in the end we are still at the starting point. The way forward will be very slow. In an age of cultural chaos each will have to find his own salvation. That is why, education in the true sense of the word, is so very important, and why in India now a complete revolution in educational method is needed. In the process of overloading our children with a multitude of facts to be learnt parrot fashion, we are completely killing initiative and imagination, the very qualities which are needed to deal with the problems confronting India today. The emphasis should be on teaching children to think for themselves, to question, to discover, to give a free rein to their unlimited curiosity, so that they develop into adults who are flexible and capable to taking decisions and acting independently.

When I was in Japan I was struck by the happy compromise the Japanese have reached between modernity and the traditional modes of life. In the offices and factories they had adopted all the best methods of western efficiency and speed, but at home they return to the ancient ways—graceful and slow—which have existed for centuries. I am not trying to glorify the old, nor have I any doubt that a lot of adaptation is necessary. There must not be thoughtless rejection. In a world which is reduced increasingly to a drab uniformity in dress, food and manners and customs, it seems to me that we should take great care to preserve all that is valuable in our way of life. The new should be questioned before being accepted. The yardstick with which we measure has to be marked by universal values. I want the ancient Indian culture to be subjected to this test. In the not-so-distant future I can conceive that the individual's confrontation with reality will not be through any particular national tradition, as it usually is now, but through universal ideas and concepts. Man will have access to a tremendous store of knowledge and aesthetic experience from which to draw and individual artists may find that they are most strongly influenced by a culture quite alien to their own. I do not think this will matter. What is important is that both the cultural statement and the appreciation should be genuine. Acknowledged liking for film magazines and pop music is better than sham preference for a high-brow weekly and Bach fugues. Although I should try to cultivate and try to improve my taste for more enduring forms until I do come to genuinely enjoy them, my reactions must be meaningful for me, and not the *ersatz* froth which in many people simulates real understanding.

Living in a large city in India today inevitably means that a great many of the aspects of life are non-Indian. I know that my Indianness is to some extent being eroded. I do not really regret this. It is in any case unavoidable, and then the whole texture of life becomes richer and more varied. But in India as a whole, the present ways will continue for many years, along traditional lines, with the conservatives fighting a long, determined rear-guard action. For me, it is not a question of modernity or tradition, but of seeking an improved quality in living for the individual, and for society. What is good in the old ways and the new must be preserved, what is harmful must be renounced. We must build upon the rock of 'Indianness' a superstructure in which the best of our tradition is combined with what is valid for us from other cultures. Thus society evolves by a continued process of rejection and assimilation.

It will be those who accept the present unthinkingly, closing their minds to the new challenges, who will have the greatest mental and spiritual conflicts. I have not been to Africa, but I have been told by many who have, that on the whole the Africans, with perhaps a lighter burden to carry from the past, have faced the problems of the twentieth century more energetically than we in Asia, who are more deeply rooted in the past. It will be an efficient society, freed from shackles of outworn custom which will be able to provide a richer and fuller life for its citizens. To be forward looking and open-minded, retaining what is best in our national heritage, but with curiosity and awareness for what is new, is the real challenge of our cultural life today.

How much Indian am I then? I eat, dress, talk and often think and feel as an Indian. But a part of me which feels the necessity for radical changes in Indian life, is entirely open and is subject to diverse non-Indian influences. I shall accept those which will bring greater sanity, greater humanity and greater happiness. I shall try to change myself and help in changing India in that direction and in that process if I lose a certain element of traditional Indianness in me, I shall have no regrets. I am an Indian who is trying to be a man.

PART THREE

IDEOLOGICAL QUEST

Chapter I

"My life is my message."—Gandhi

I had never been very enthusiastic about Gandhism. That was not surprising since I was brought up in Bengal, a province where the weight of his influence was felt the least. In fact, during a quarter of a century of Gandhi's virtual domination of the Indian National Congress only twice was there any significant challenge to his ideas and policies and on both eccasions the leaders of Bengal played a prominent role. Moreover, in the environment in which I grew up there was considerable reservation about Gandhi's ideas and later, open hostility towards him.

At the same time however there prevailed a peculiar ambiguity in the attitude towards Gandhi. As a political leader and a man, he evoked a schizophrenic reaction. One could differ violently with him on political or economic questions but it was impossible to overlook the magnificent contribution he made towards India's struggle for freedom, and his simplicity, warmheartedness and devotion were qualities which won him admirers all over the world. It was difficult, when faced with such a complex and fascinating personality, to maintain a really balanced approach, and amidst the din of opposition to his political ideas it was easy to underestimate his basic qualities. On the other hand, many, dazzled by his magnetism, failed to see the errors in his political judgments. I wanted not to be guilty of either of these misconceptions. As I grew up I tried to arrive at a fair and objective appraisal of Gandhi's ideas. This seemed to be important for two reasons. In the first place he presented a typically Indian solution to the problems which faced our country and secondly, he had enormous influence on the mass of Indian people. One could not possibly plan for the future without taking into account the legacy he had left behind. It was he who made the Indian struggle something more than a struggle of intellectuals. He carried it into the remotest villages so that a whole nation was actively involved in the fight.

Whatever reservations individuals might have had regarding

his ideas, his sincerity was never questioned. But in 1947 disturbing doubts regarding even this aspect of his character began to trouble me. Why, I asked myself, did he not actively and openly oppose the partition of India, an act which would mean the complete destruction of everything he had worked for through the years? He had fasted more than twenty times during his life; sometimes on issues which seemed quite trivial to others, but he justified them on the basis of the call of his "inner voice." Whether one approved of the method or not, that was his way of expressing himself. Why did he not consider partition of the country to be an occasion for fasting? Why did his "inner voice" remain silent? Anybody with the slightest acquaintance with his life and activities would say the issue of partition was of very great importance for him. Was it then because he had been forced to accept that the idea of partition was the logical consequence of his own failure to solve the Hindu-Muslim problem? Did he, as a hard-headed realist, come around to the view that partition was a temporary solution to the communal problem and abandon his own ideas since they had no popular support? Or, did he think that the combined strength of the British government, the Muslim League and the Congress right wing, added to the deterioration in the political situation after the communal rioting, was too powerful a force to be put into disarray by such a gesture as his fasting?

I have put these questions to many devoted Gandhians but have never managed to get really satisfactory answers. To me, his attitude seemed to indicate his failure both as a political leader and as a man. He did not prove a strong enough saint to pursue his own truth even when the whole world went against him and as a political leader, when political events were leading to a climax, he chose to remain passive and allowed events to take their own course. Feeling helpless he kept himself away from the centre of power at the most crucial hour and devoted himself to the secondary problems of communal harmony in far away places. During this period my disenchantment with him was complete.

Looking back it seems his fate could not have been otherwise. He was caught in the web of his own contradictions.

When Gandhi became prominent on the Indian political scene after the first world war, both the constitutional struggle and attempts at armed revolt had proved a failure. After the massacre of Amritsar in 1919 the whole country was roused and a great urge was felt for political action. Gandhi's technique of non-violent non-cooperation captured the imagination of the people because for an unarmed nation it was the only possible way to continue the struggle. Gandhi argued that Britain, a small country, could maintain her hold on the vast sub-continent only with the co-operation of the Indian people. If every one decided not to co-operate, he said, their rule would end. This was simple and captivating logic. He was able to explain to the peasantry in simple mythological language, which they understood, what "Swaraj" (self-government) would mean and he soon transformed the talking, petition-making body of the Congress into a dynamic mass organization with its network spread throughout the country. He had a genius for conceiving and carrying out the village industries programme to provide economic sustenance for the political movement. All these factors, combined with the personality of a leader, who was saintly in the best traditions of Indian culture, helped to transform the whole nationalist movement.

The widespread success of his work influenced Gandhi to promise "Swaraj" within one year in 1920. But it took 27 years to attain Dominion Status and that in a divided country. He misjudged the character and strength of the opponent, the British government; instead of maintaining the pragmatic nature of the movement he instilled into it a number of his own philosophical and social fads and fancies; he wanted to solve the communal problem with an added dose of religiosity and although he was able to keep his hold over Congress by yielding to the radical political pressure within the organization from time to time, right till the end he remained quite impervious to the influence of modern social and economic thinking.

Thus, in spite of his unique political contribution, with the passing of a quarter century, which brought about great changes in India and in the world, he became more and more an anachronism. It was not surprising that his closest political collaborators like Sardar Patel and Dr. Rajendra Prasad and even his political "heir" Jawaharlal Nehru, deserted him when they were confronted with the responsibility of grappling with the problems of mid-twentieth century India. The India that they helped to build up after Gandhi's death had very little relevance to Gandhi's ideas. The most curious thing is that these leaders were never tired of repeating *ad nauseum* how profoundly they were influenced by Gandhi and how in their activities they drew their inspiration from him. This dissociation of their words from actual reality has created an unhealthy psychological and moral climate in the country. Their attitude has contributed much to the confused thinking on fundamental issues which prevails so extensively in India.

It is true that a section of Gandhians, led by J. B. Kripalani, dissociated themselves from the "ruling Gandhians" and criticised many aspects of their policies. After the first general elections they merged themselves with the Socialist Party but could not evolve any distinctive Gandhian political attitudes. Today their influence is almost non-existent.

However, the more orthodox of the non-political disciples of Gandhi, led by Vinoba Bhave, started the Bhoodan movement which initially took the country by storm, but with its piecemeal, isolated and non-political approach it was successful only up to a point and then it stagnated. The notion that "islands of virtue" could be built and sustained upon a rapidly changing socio-economic scene, without being allied to any broader political movement proved to be mistaken one. It tended to become a moralist-religious movement in a society where morals were becoming increasingly confused and where deeper religious feelings suffered continuous erosion. In any discussion on Gandhism it is important to remember that the India of 1920 which threw up the phenomenal figure of Gandhi no longer exists. What is more, it is going to be a different kind of India, whether one may like it or not, with people having different attitudes and values. In this context I have examined some of the fundamental ideas which Gandhi championed.

The first and foremost was the issue of non-violence. There were two aspects of the problem. First, as a teachnique for the freedom struggle and secondly, as a method having universal application under all circumstances. As a technique of struggle it had wide acceptance. Even those who believed in the usefulness of violence in the struggle against the British government, were not in a position to achieve anything substantial in that direction, because the procuring and maintenance of arms in a sufficient quantity to pose a decisive threat to the British government, was simply an impossibility. Therefore, the non-violent method was the only feasible one in normal times. While such people were with Gandhi in the non-violent struggle, they were prepared to take up arms if and when there were opportunities for it. This happened to some extent during the "Quit India" movement in the country and in the I.N.A. struggle outside.

Gandhi believed in non-violence in the absolute sense. There was an infinite amount of controversy among my friends on this point. Actually very few people went whole-hogging with Gandhi on this issue. Can a country be defended against armed aggression by non-violent means or can law and order be preserved when a riotous mob gets the upper hand?

The 'Gandhian' government of India answered the questions by ear-marking nearly half of its budget for military expenditure and by employing armed police against aggressive but unarmed demonstrations on innumerable occasions, causing death and injuries. After the Chinese aggression some devout Gandhians wanted to organize a march of "peace soldiers" to Peking but this caused only embarrassed amusement in the country.

What then does non-violence mean in Free India? I have not found anything in the Indian system which distinguishes it from any of those in liberal, democratic societies in Europe or North America where all major decisions are taken by peaceful, non-violent elections. There seems to be no specific Gandhian contribution to parliamentary life in India as it exists today. It is true that Jayaprakash Narayan has presented a blueprint from the Gandhian angle as to what a democratic set-up ought to be but it rejected the parliamentary system and the plan has found no support in the country.

There was, it is true, Gandhian emphasis on decentralisation of economic and political power, but this is not a typically Gandhian concept. Many socialist thinkers consider it to be the basis of democratic life. Even Yugoslav communists, for instance, have made a significant contribution to the theory and practice of decentralization.

Gandhi's stress on small-scale, village industries, shorn of all *mystique*, is of immense practical value. In a country where agriculture in itself cannot sustain an ever increasing population and large scale industry is not in a position to absorb the surplus, the adoption of small industries on an extensive scale to offer employment is the logic of economic science, Gandhi or no Gandhi.

This emphasis on cottage industry was linked with his general conception of life. By temperament and thinking, he was opposed to industrialization and all its accompanying ills. This was an aspect of Gandhi's thought which was destined to be rejected. In fact, it was already rejected by Bose and Nehru. It is interesting that two of the most powerful and significant personalities in India—Gandhi and Tagore—were not modernists. They were pessimists regarding industrialization. They had the occasion to witness the decline of western civilization as manifested during the first world war. The whole liberal concepts of 'automatic progress' and 'human perfectibility' were shattered. The rise of Bolshevism, Fascism and Nazism and the steady drift towards another world war had only confirmed their doubts about the efficacy of the western way of life. They cherished more than ever the traditional values and tried to enshrine them in the institutions they built up. Their opposition to the modernistic trends in Indian life, however formidable they might have been, was however doomed to failure just as the romantic revolts in western countries had failed in the past. Many of their criticisms of industrialization are valid, but the very fact that industrialization alone is capable of offering increasingly large quantities of diversified goods and cultural amenities, in which the common man is deeply interested, makes it an inevitable development. In such a situation there are three alternatives : to plunge headlong into change without much concern about non-material aspects of human life; to accept the inevitable and to humanize the process as much as possible; and, finally, to oppose it. Gandhi was opposed to large-scale industrialization. Support for this policy even from the peasantry would have progressively declined. Being a believer of modernism, Gandhi's attitude in this respect was completely unacceptable to me.

Another of Gandhi's ideas, which was opposed by the progressive elements in the country was his conception of trusteeship. Against common ownership himself, he wanted the continuance of private ownership, but with the owners functioning as trustees of their property, seeing to the legitimate interests of all connected with their particular enterprise. Gandhi had infinite faith in the possibility of a 'change of heart' on the part of capitalists and landlords who would minimize their own share of profits so that all might benefit. That certain members of the owner-class might have followed such a course of action is feasible enough, but to make such a theory part of a total social policy seems to be placing too much faith in human nature. If indeed Gandhi's expectations in this direction had been fulfilled would not Birla, one of his most enthusiastic followers and a leading industrialist, have been a pioneer in putting Gandhi's ideas into practice? This, it need hardly be said, did not happen.

However, the activities carried out during his efforts to implement this policy, brought him many supporters amongst the capitalist class, who saw in his theories a lesser evil than the appropriation which would likely to be followed under a socialist regime. By a slight shift in the emphasis of his arguments it was easy to show that Gandhi was a supporter of capitalism, while ignoring the responsibilities which he maintained should accompany ownership. It was not surprising that one of the consequences of this confusion of thought followed when Sardar Patel, one of Gandhi's closest collaborators, became in the post-independence era a great defender of big business in the country. Such was the nebulous character of the trusteeship philosophy however, that it was difficult to indicate anything in Sardar Patel's policy which was specifically anti-Gandhian, yet a number of prominent Gandhians like Kripalani and others did go to the length of dissociating themselves from it.

From a socialist point of view, there were genuine doubts whether, after independence, the collaboration between the classes, which would result from the trusteeship idea, was a state of affairs which should be encouraged. Even if it were possible to maintain it, it was a moot question whether it would be in the best interests of the peasant and working classes, who would be more likely to benefit from class struggle.

Has then the Gandhian spirit shown any significant influence upon the workings of capitalists within the country during the years in which India has been independent? Perhaps in some areas there has been certain amount of enlightenment. Tatas from the very beginning have had a fairly good record for providing social amenities and for the distribution of bonuses among their workers. But most of the greatest tycoons of the West are also known for their philanthropic activities. The same monopolistic tendencies exist in India and have created a tremendous concentration of economic power which is essentially undemocratic in character. At the same time a considerable section of the capitalist class are loudly evoking the name of Gandhi to justify their way of life. Many of his ideas are distorted in the process but that there was scope for distortion cannot be denied. After all, he often lived and ultimately died in the house of one of India's greatest industrialists. There was no question of his rejection of the lords of wealth.

Has Gandhi then nothing to offer to the younger gneeration? He had, I think, much that was inspiring in his life which has great relevance to present day conditions, not only in India, but all over the world. In the first place he was one of the few to insist upon the true worth and dignity of every man however poor or however low a place he occupied in the social structure, and to give practical expression to his belief. His struggle against untouchability will continue to have meaning for all those who fight inequality in whatever field. Heaven knows inspiration is necessary in this country, surely one of the most caste-ridden societies in existence. All over the world, wherever man is set against man because of race or creed, there will arise someone in whom the Gandhian spirit still lives on, to speak of the brotherhood of all mankind.

Secondly, the importance which Gandhi placed upon love as a factor in both individual and social life, acts as a guiding principle to any one who wants to construct something worthwhile in the realm of human relationships, whether public or private. As I grew older I found that love was a sure means of human transformation, bestowing at the same time an enduring quality on the changes it brings about. Since this is true in terms of individuals it is reasonable to suppose that it therefore has social implications. Nevertheless one has frequently to make compromises with reality. Often love is not enough; love, for Gandhi could not solve the Hindu-Muslim problem. However it seems clear that a society where love is a dominating influence, will be superior to one where selfishness and greed are prevailing motives. Wherever men are labouring to build up a way of life which is a true fulfillment for all, Gandhi's successes and failures will continue to provide valid lessons for years to come.

Thirdly, the technique of *satyagraha* which he introduced as one of the chief weapons of the freedom struggle will continue to have direct relevance in India and the world at large. In those societies where there are full democratic and constitutional rights to persuade the majority, many people dismiss this method as undemocratic. While admitting that in a democracy minority opinion should have sufficient patience and persistence to convince the majority, it sometimes happens that in a nation's life problems arise which cannot wait indefinitely to get the sanction of the majority. In such circumstances the adoption of the technique of satyagraha as a part of the propaganda drive could usefully be used. This has happened not only in India, but also in Britain where civil disobedience has played a prominent role in the demonstrations organized by the Campaign for Nuclear Disarmament and in the United States during the struggles of the Negro people for integration. It is true that this method should be used only in extreme cases, but it could reasonably become part of the normal process for persuasion in a democratic society when burning issues arise which cannot be left to the slow and dilatory process of normal democratic persuasion. People in every country of the world derive great encouragement and inspiration from Gandhi's experiments with satyagraha.

What appeals to me most in Gandhi's life is his insistence upon simplicity, which from a modern point of view would be considered ascetic. His hatred of snobbery, his emphasis on the bare necessities of living his refusal to make a fetish of goods and his delight in spontaneity of feelings are meaningful directives to the society which we see emerging in India with its pursuit of material wealth, where artificiality is on the increase and where to be simple will soon be equated with deficiency of intelligence.

These attitudes of Gandhi reflected the inner richness which came from his recognition of the fundamental realities of life in India, and from his unceasing efforts to do something about them. That inevitably gave him a different yardstick by which to judge issues. One of the stories which I like most about him is the one where he is said to have defied all the protocol of the court of the British Empire by appearing at an audience with King George V in the loincloth. That a man is to be judged by his qualities and not by the clothes he wears, is something which many people forget. In our every day life it is the inner reality rather than the exterior appearance which should be given greater importance. The India of Gandhi's dream would have won the respect of the world not by the length of her ambassadorial cars and the grandeur of its embassies but by the simple dignity of a splendid vision combined with efforts and achievements.

It is the spirit of Gandhi which will continue to have eternal appeal rather than his poetic exaggerations. It is not an easy task to continue to hold on to those ideas which have significance for our generation, but I certainly think the effort to be worth waking.

In the task of transforming India into an industrial nation it would seem that the ideas of Gandhi have little relevance. Nevertheless, his emphasis on the basic values by which men live, and his efforts to express them in his own life, will always remain an inspiration to those who would wish to see India take an honoured place in the world.

Gandhi was a unique individual. In his life he enabled ordinary people to surpass themselves. After his death he looks down from many a pedestal upon those who venerate him for his saintliness, but have no intention of following in his footsteps.

CHAPTER II

The Communist Party is "the intelligence, the honour and the conscience of our epoch".—Lenin

It was those same feelings of personal inadequacy, which made me throw myself into the nationalist movement with such youthful fervour, which later attracted me towards the socialist ideal. Feeling myself to be the victim of unfair discrimination I wanted a world where the unattractive, the handicapped, the disabled would be given a just deal by society. Both materially and psychologically, for me, the egalitarian ideals of socialism satisfied a deeply-felt personal, physical and emotional need. For many, socialism is a cerebral activity not affecting the heart. It is for them "a thing apart", I wanted to make socialism "my whole existence."

This did not mean, however, that my emotions were given a free rein, with no intellectual control. My head buzzed with questions. I wanted to find my place in the universal scheme of things and soon realised that could be accomplished only if I embarked upon an ideological quest. It is not surprising that initially this search led along the path towards communism.

Before the war, facts about the Soviet Union were not widely known in India and had made no great impact upon the imagination of the Indian people. Although the Communist Party of India had been formed in the early 'twenties, communist ideas had appealed to a comparatively small section of the intelligentsia. Banned for a long time by the British government, the communists had yet been able to extend their influence over a section of the working class and the student population, but they had kept themselves apart from the broad stream of the nationalist movement and all its struggles. During the popular front days of the 'thirties they had come into the Congress but their spirited rejection of "Quit India" movement in 1942 and their open collaboration with the British government thereafter, had completely estranged them from other sections of political opinion in India. I felt a strong antipathy towards the Communist Party because of their anti-national policy.

During the war however the news of the heroic struggle of the Soviet people against German invasion began to pour into the country and for the first time our attention was focussed on the Soviet Union and its system of government. During the latter half of the war, having full right of political action, the Communist Party brought out cheap editions of the writings of Marx, Engels, Lenin and Stalin and by the end of the war Marxism and the Soviet Union were no longer a closed book in India.

My fascination for the Soviet system started with my admiration for the Soviet people's valiant struggle against the Nazis. It seemed that unlike some other European nations, they had something to fight for. Of the many books that I read at that time, two books made a deep impression "Mission to Moscow" by Joseph Davies, in which a representative of the U.S.A., a capitalist country, provided first-hand information about the situation inside the Soviet Union, and "Mother Russia" by Maurice Hindus, depicting the tragic grandeur of the Soviet people's patriotic struggle which exerted a greater emotional impact. The innumerable books, booklets, novels and magazines that I read and a number of films that I saw convinced me that an ideal society was in the process of construction in the Soviet Union. Of course, there were defects and difficulties but that was understandable. The direction in which the Soviet leaders were taking the country was the right one—towards the establishment of a socialist society. Moreover, the Soviet Union was the first country in which the working people had taken over the political power of the State, in order to reconstruct society in a fundamental way. That was a gigantic task and it seemed to me that everybody in the world who had the cause of socialism at heart, should support such a mighty venture.

Soon I came to accept many of the concepts of Marxism—the class struggle, the necessity for a revolutionary seizure of power, the expropriation of expropriators, the international solidarity of the working people. Since my rejection of the existing society was complete, there was a vacuum in my mind and in my frantic search for the answers to the problems of life, I did not find any other single philosophy which provided such coherent and comprehensive answers. Not that I understood or even agreed with everything, but the vacuum became filled with a vision of socialism, finding its expression in the Soviet state, and the rudiments of Marxism served as a rough guide to action. My temperament too, was suited to communism : I had a strong impulse towards total commitment, a craving for intellectual abstraction and, I suspect, a strain of ruthlessness in the pursuit of my ideal. Communism was slowly emerging as a creed to which I could dedicate myself completely.

In spite of this intellectual attraction however, it never occurred to me to join the Communist Party, which, by its policies had alienated too much of my sympathy. Nevertheless, had my thinking continued to develop along these channels it seems likely that I should in the end have become a member.

Then the pilgrim's progress came to an unexpected and sudden halt. One day I returned from the library with a copy of Koestler's "The Yogi and the Commissar"—a collection of brilliant essays. Here I read with growing consternation about highly differential wages in the Soviet Union; the privileges of the hierarchy and the reactionary tendencies towards social questions like divorce, abortion, juvenile deliquency and homosexuality, which I thought could not be equated with my conception of socialism.

For me the appeal of communism had been basically an ethical one, of human solidarity. I have never been a believer in the equality advocated by Bernard Shaw who wanted equal wages for every one, but I did think that the differentials in wages in a socialist society should be as little as possible. I could find no justification for the fact that in the Soviet Union there were greater differences between the lowest and the highest paid workers in the administration or the army, than existed in the capitalist countries. I learnt further, that according to Stalin, equality was a petty-bourgeois aberration. It seemed obvious that if privilege and discrimination were allowed in by the back door, then however fair a name a system went under, it was not the one to which I could owe my allegiance.

For the first time I became aware that a whole body of progressive criticism existed regarding the Soviet system. I became eager to know what they had to say. It was difficult to separate this from the flood of literature stemming from reactionary forces who hurled lies and slander at the first "workers' state" in an effort to finish her off. Soon the Indian market was flooded with conflicting interpretations and evaluations of the Soviet Union and communism in general.

Now, although I passionately wanted a way of life and a philosophy to live by and communism seemed to provide that, I did not want to acquire a faith by sacrificing truth. I had begun by asking questions and had no intention of giving up that habit. I was prepared to go anywhere to get my data and would accept them if they were proved authentic. It did not matter where they came from and how they affected my own cherished "theories". I wanted a way of life based on rationality, which would give every human being equal worth and which would provide me with a code of personal conduct.

In pursuit of a real understanding of communism I have met and talked with communists of many countries but for me perhaps the most fruitful encounter was with one of the brightest young men in the Communist Party of India. The son of a High Court judge, he was a brilliant student and debater in the university; he went to Cambridge for higher studies and then he "disappeared" for sometime behind the Iron Curtain, before returning to India as full time party activist. He came close to the central party leadership.

It was in the beginning of 1956 that we began a series of meetings in New Delhi where we systematically discussed communism in all its aspects, particularly those questions which used to bother me most about the Soviet Union : lack of democracy within the Communist Party, bureaucratic control of the economy, the idolatory of Stalin, cultural regimentation and the police terror. As a loyal and brilliant communist he used to explain away each question patiently or justify each and every facet of Soviet communism, because at that time it was not customary for the communists to talk about the "mistakes committed in the past". He even had, I distinctly remember, a beautiful metaphorical explanation of the poem, which was published in Pravda :

"O Great Stalin, O leader of the people
Thou bringest man to birth . . ."

Then, out of the blue, a bombshell burst in the midst of our discussions—Khrushchev's secret report to the twentieth congress of the Soviet Communist Party. When I read it I found to my surprise that many of the points that I had mentioned to my communist friend had their place there—the only difference being, that this time they were mentioned by the General Secretary of the CPSU and I was, at best, a petit-bourgeois fogy and at worst "a professional slanderer of the Soviet Union in the payroll of CIA."

I felt on top of the world in the company of Comrade Khrushchev and my friend was left far below, completely confused and lost.

After that when I met him I suggested that we should not discuss the Soviet Union at all.

"I have come," I said, "with only one question and that is a personal one. By any objective standard, you are more intelligent that I am; from experience and study you know far more about the Soviet Union than I shall ever know. Yet in spite of all that, how is it that I seem to have arrived at a more correct appraisal of the Soviet situation than you?"

For once his communist creed did not provide him with a ready answer—his confidence had been badly shaken. That quintessence of human wisdom, manifest in communist philosophy, the power of which makes the communists "the will and instrument of history", had suddenly deserted him. Yet in the answer to this question was hidden the whole confused intellectual and psychological make-up of communism.

At last he said. "Obviously we have been misinformed in the past. On the basis of this new knowledge we will have to rethink and revalue many things." That however was not an answer to my question.

"I think the reason is simple," I said. "Your assessment was faulty because you have ceased to be scientific." He was shocked. How could the inheritors of Marx and Engels, the fathers of Scientific Socialism, be unscientific?

"Scientific method implies," I added, "that one has to get raw facts, as they are, and evolve a theory to interpret or explain those facts. One can, of course, start with a hypothesis and subject it to empirical verification. But you communists have stopped doing that. You have a strict and rigid doctrine Marxism-Leninism. You not only see reality through the coloured glass of your doctrine but you also overlook those phenomena which do not fit in with your theories, instead of adjusting your theories to those realities. This, I submit, is a religious rather than a scientific approach. That is why, in spite of your having a better tools and knowledge than I, your appraisal of the Soviet Union has shown a serious error of judgment."

He was naturally unwilling to accept this explanation but he could not provide a more satisfactory one of his own.

So I went on to develop the point. "Scientific Socialism was developed in the nineteenth century from the best of German philosophy, English economics and French sociology, and became the mightiest intellectual weapon of the working class movement. Gradually for various reasons this theory began to assume, especially in Russia, an increasingly rigid form because it was taken for granted that since all basic truths that are worth knowing have been known through Marxism, there was no question of improving or revising them. There was no more any possibility of questioning the fundamental assumptions because they had acquired the character of "divine revelations". So when a communist argues a case today he finds final justification in a suitable quotation from Marx, Engels, Lenin or Stalin. This process might be defective as an intellectual discipline but it has one advantage. In this age of crumbling faiths, Marxism-Leninism offers a substitute for religion. Its wide appeal is understandable because it has a veneer of scientific sophistication, it takes interest in social problems, but above all it offers a faith and a way of life for intellectuals like you.

"Here the question arises : at what cost should one adopt such a faith ? I once knew a charming Catholic nun, who was very intelligent and well-informed. One day I met her in the street and asked her whether I could see her some time. "What for ?" she asked suspiciously. "To talk about education, culture, and religion, if you like," I replied. "Oh ! no," she said. "I am told you are a communist." Then she added the words which still ring in my ears : "You will ensnare my innocent mind."

"Like that nun you have an overriding, maybe unconscious, psychological drive to keep your mind 'innocent'—to feel warm and cosy in the bosom of Marxist faith. You do not want any disturbing light to come in and upset everything. You must have heard all the adverse criticism concerning the Soviet Union before, but you put up a psychological censorship against it. As a result you feel happy because it gives you the feeling of comradeship with the communists in all parts of the world; you feel in sympathy with the exploited people everywhere and you have the magnificent feeling of being on the crest of the wave of the future. It is, I know, a very intoxicating feeling, one of the finest that we can experience in this world of misery and wickedness, doubts and uncertainties.

"You have given your love to the Soviet Union. I have no objection to that, but do not tell me that you want to seek truth and that you are scientific in your method or that you live the truth. Like that gentle nun I would not expect you to give me the truth about the object you love.

"All of us have selective perception; we want to see only those things which please us and are inclined to reject unpleasant truths or subject them to a process of rationalization. I try my best to know the truth even if it is unpleasant. I want to know the truth about the Soviet Union and about every thing else not simply to satisfy idle curiosity, but to live the truth."

My friend was silent. Intelligent, perceptive as he was, in relation to the central passion of his life, his intelligence and perception had failed him. Communism, it seems, puts blinkers over the eyes of its adherents.

I remember the Indian communist leader A. K. Gopalan, who after a visit to the Soviet Union in the early 'fifties, called that country on his return "a heaven on earth". Six years later I, too, went there, and what I saw, convinced me that those who said it would take at least fifteen years before West European standards were achieved, were correct in their prophecy. The Soviet Union is still far from heaven. Now, was Gopalan so blind that he did not see the obvious, or was he consciously telling untruths, to impress the Indian people? The perpetration of falsehood for expediency's sake is within the accepted code of Leninist behaviour, which demands the acceptance of its own particular form of truth as infallible, and yet indulges in the calculated lie. This is a frequent result of the communist capacity for double-thinking.

Marxist 'intelligence' as developed in the Soviet Union and other communist countries assumes that all the fundamental truths about man, society and universe have been known and that what is now needed is a process of elaboration upon these truths. Any new knowledge which does not conform with the basic insights of Marxism-Leninism cannot be accepted. Like medieval Christian theology present day Marxism-Leninism puts reality on a Procustean-bed. All ideas must be forced into a rigid pattern. The unfettered pursuit of truth has no place within the system; such an attitude is contemptuously dismissed as "bourgeois objectivism".

This same rigidity can be seen in the communist attitude towards the arts. All the new and significant experiments in literature, painting and music are branded as "alien" to working class ideology. Consequently after 1890 some of the major developments in the artistic world have made no impact on the official Marxist aesthetic sensibility. The entire non-Marxist creative endeavour is virtually rejected as though it had never existed. Their piece-meal efforts to recognise some "progressive" artists quickly draws them into incredible confusion.

Perhaps one's opposition to such a dogmatic approach would not have been so great, if the Marxists had been able to produce anything of outstanding value within their limited framework, but socialist realism has put a strangehold on artistic expression.

To comprehend the infinite complexity of the human condition in the latter half of the twentieth century it is essential to take into account the whole gamut of human knowledge. By bringing about artificial divisions in this knowledge, the communists have impoverished the human spirit.

By any standard my communist friend is a 'fine' person sensitive, generous, self-sacrificing and disciplined. Throughout the world the Communist Parties are able to draw some of the finest people into their ranks, but this is no real criterion by which a movement should be judged. After all, even the Nazi movement recruited many devoted and loyal workers, especially in its early days. The greatness of an individual or of a movement cannot be measured purely by sacrifice but also by the capacity to discern the right goal and the path which leads to it.

However, the common man's appraisal of communism is made from its activities (in those countries where the communists are in the opposition) and from first-hand knowledge of the communists themselves, which is often favourable. They carry much 'honour'—they identify themselves with the sufferings of the people and uphold their cause often at great cost to themselves. The disciplined and dedicated activities of the communists in many parts of the world constitute some of the finest chapters of contemporary history.

With the transformation of communist 'intelligence' with its capacity for creative endeavour, into dogmatic, unscientific acceptance of creed, the 'honour' is no longer properly utilized. That honour largely remains is unquestionable, but honour is not enough unless impelled by the ability to subject one's actions to the searchlight of objective criteria.

The communist movement is the conscience of our epoch, said Lenin. Here again, there is a dichotomy between the expressed theory and its translation into action. If conscience is that sensitivity, that awareness which would judge an issue on the basis of some absolute moral standards, then communists have a dangerous schism in their conscience. The schism is most sharply reflected through the works of communist artists in non-communist countries. They are quite rightly indignant about the exploitation, suffering and misery of the working people in their countries; they help to raise the banner of revolt and they even indicate a vision of a juster world. Yet they remain silent when wrongs are committed in communist countries. Either they do not recognise the obvious facts or they try to explain them away and in that process their conscience becomes muted. The party, which functions as a jealous mistress, dictates the line and asks artists to condone and applaud its acts. The right of individuals to judge an issue on its own merits is not allowed within the communist movement. So I found that on every question which has troubled the human conscience—colonial freedom, disarmament, respect for human and democratic rights, the communists have made compromises and their artists and intellectuals have never openly come out against the policies of their governments and parties. If any attempt is made in this direction their acts are immediately branded as counter-revolutionary. Yet the conscience of an epoch finds its most sensitive expression through the works of artists who can express man's deepest yearnings and highest values. The great artist with his heightened sensibility could, through his work, become in Shelley's words the "unacknowledged legislator", but in communist countries such a possibility is ruled out, for the politicians, guided by their interests and expediency, decide all issues and impose their decisions upon every section of society.

So I came to realise, that with the world divided into two opposing factions, armed with their own ideologies, backed by ever increasing nuclear power, survival was becoming a questionable possibility in the life of man. Some objective principle by which international actions could be tested was an urgent necessity. The attitude of mind which condemns Suez but condones Hungary is as untenable as that which defends Suez and condemns Hungary; as is the credulousness which seems to imagine that in some way the fall-out from Russian 50-megaton bomb is less maleficent than that from the American explosions.

How I ask myself could I join a movement which despite all the attraction it held for me, took no principled stand on any outstanding issue because of the pulls and pressures of big power politics ? The common cry of humanity in protest against annihilation was growing in volume. There must have been millions in communist countries who would have liked to join, but their voice was stifled. One heard of shrill, heretical voices, but they soon faded out.

The things became increasingly clear in my mind. There would be no hope for mankind unless within short time it was able to transform itself fundamentally. Secondly, communism with its world wide commitment and vested interest was too much tied up with the past to be able to extricate itself from the situation which was leading us towards extinction. Its old framework of thinking was unable to contain the new complexities or offer a sane solution. To avert a nuclear holocaust the Soviet leaders are being compelled to revise their dogmas, and if this trend continues there will be hardly anything specifically communist left in the process of time. While those who continue to follow the dogmatic line will constitute the gravest danger to human civilization.

To be able to find my place in the world, to discover my identity I wanted to belong to some organisation which would reflect the highest intelligence of our time, the most sensitive conscience and the greatest honour. I could not find it in the communist movement.

CHAPTER III

"Socialism is at bottom a question of ethics or morals. It has mainly to do with the relationship which should exist between a man and his fellows."—Keir Hardie.

During the freedom struggle I drew my main political inspiration from my uncle, Subhas. For to me he was not only a fighter for freedom but he also had a clear conception as to how Free India should be built. Consequently his ideas did not become outdated with the attainment of independence and he continued to remain one of the most significant influences in my life.

I felt that he was right in his assertion that Leftism in Free India would mean the struggle for and the establishment of a socialist society and I was sympathetic towards his pragmatic attitude. "No standpoint or theory in socio-political affairs can be the last word in human wisdom," he said. "Socio-political theories and institutions of the modern nations are the product of their history, environment and needs. Time must elapse before they could be declared to be successful and in the meantime we should not mortgage our intellect anywhere. My own attitude has always been that India's task is to work out a synthesis of what is useful and good in the different movements that we see today."

This was an approach which appealed to me and I still consider it to be sound.

In the heyday of the 'pink period' of the thirties on one occasion Nehru expressed the opinion that "the choice before the world today is between some form of communism and some form of fascism and I am all for the former, that is, communism." Bose promptly countered this by saying, "Unless we are at the end of the process of evolution or unless we deny evolution altogether, there is no reason to hold that our choice is restricted to two alternatives."

The essence of his social thinking was that "we in India would like to have a progressive system which will fulfil the social needs of the people and will be based on national sentiment. In other words, it will be a synthesis of nationalism and socialism." For such an attitude many of his political opponents accused him of being a fascist but there was no truth in their allegations. Even during the war when he worked in close collaboration with the Axis powers for India's freedom, it could never be proved that through his activities he was championing Fascist ideas. Today nobody would say that socialism and nationalism are completely contradictory concepts, unless of course one equates nationalism with chauvinism or jingoism, which Bose did not.

In fact, one of his reasons for rejecting communism was that it did not appreciate the value of national sentiment. He visualised that the materialist interpretation of history as well as the anti-religious attitude of the communists would not have ready acceptance in India. He even thought that Marxism placed too much emphasis on the economic factor in human life. "We fully appreciate the importance of the economic factor which was formerly ignored," he said, "but it is not necessary to over-emphasise it." Another defect that he found in Marxist theory was that emphasis was placed on the working class to the exclusion of the peasantry, a great handicap in a country where the overwhelming majority of the population belongs to the peasant class.

Being practical by nature, he disliked the communist habit of importing wholesale ideas and methods from other countries. "While seeking light and inspiration from abroad we cannot forget we should not blindly imitate any other people and that we should assimilate what we learn elsewhere after finding out what will suit our national requirements."

Unlike Gandhi, he was a modernist. He was of the opinion that both for the raising of the standard of living of the masses and for the defence of the society it was necessary to implement a speedy process of industrialization. Again, differing from Gandhi he thought that the party which would ultimately bring the independence of the country would also have the task of bringing about socio-economic transformation. He thought that "If we are to have an economic structure of socialistic character then it follows that the political system be such as to be able to carry out that economic programme in the best possible way." Up to this point I agreed with his ideas but their further development proved to be controversial. "You cannot have a so-called democratic system if that system has to put through economic reforms on a socialistic basis." In order to do this he thought it might be necessary to have an authoritarian system of government for a temporary period.

He did not elaborate on this theory but this aspect of his thinking raised certain doubts in my mind. It was clear from the nature of the totalitarian and authoritarian governments then existing in many parts of the world, that there was an inherent tendency for their allegedly temporary character to become permanent, and the restoration of the democratic process an unrealised dream. It was of course not possible for him to have foreseen the political development which actually took place after independence. I had to formulate my own attitude towards the new government. It was obvious that the Congress government had no intention of carrying out a socialist programme. It did however give freedom of expression and association and owing to the complete predominance of the ruling party a period of political stability prevailed. In such a situation, the constant harping on revolutionary slogans by some of Bose's followers cut absolutely no ice. Any party which had adopted a revolutionary programme at that time (as did the Communist Party in 1948, in conformity with the Zhdanov Plan of the international communist movement) would have been doomed to failure. In fact, there had been no time during twentyfour years of independence when a situation had developed which could have been exploited by revolutionary groups. Even had any such development been created locally it is obvious they could not have held out long against the formidable power of the Central Government. It became clear, especially after the first general elections in 1952, that the political game would in the future only be played according to parliamentary and constitutional rules. Although at this time in 1953 I played no active part in politics, I was nevertheless in favour of the merger of a section of the Forward Bloc with the Praja Socialist Party. Prior to this there had been an unfortunate controversy in the Forward Bloc over Marxism which later split the Party; one section calling themselves Marxists, the other Subhasists. I aligned myself with the Subhasists since I could not agree with the Marxist monistic interpretation of events. Reality, it seemed, was too complex to be reduced to such dogmatic simplicity.

I had never shared the great excitement over Marxism, either for or against it. I accepted it as a part, a significant part certainly, of my intellectual heritage. I accepted those aspects of Marx's thinking which had stood the test of time and rejected those which had not. He was, I consider, one of the most brilliant thinkers of the nineteenth century. The trouble was that some of his disciples made him into a demi-god and his opponents into semi-devil. Both, it seemed to me, were mistaken.

Among the Marxists themselves there was hardly any agreement as to what Marxism actually was. However, in the popular mind Marxism was equated with the complex ideas, beliefs and practices championed by the communists of the Third International, founded by Lenin and directed from Moscow.

To my mind only the writings of Marx and Engels constituted "authentic" Marxism. After nearly hundred years I think it is possible for an objective observer to find out what is valid in their writings, and what is not. For instance, the prophecies that Marx made regarding certain aspects of capitalism in his time—its tendencies towards centralization, concentration of capital, the growth of monopoly and contraction of the free market itself, fulfilled themselves in a remarkable way.

It is equally obvious that he underestimated the influence of democratic factors, progressive taxation, deficit financing and the whole series of measures that capitalism adopted in order to survive. Therefore, the political calculation of Marx that the middle class would progressively disappear and that the increasing pauperisation of the working class would cause a revolutionary explosion, proved wrong. I find the efforts to 'justify' Marx and Engels even in these spheres quite fruitless.

However, Marx's analysis of property and social relations is illuminating, his initiation of scientific sociology, his conception of the whole man and his deep concern for human alienation, which he believed could be overcome by creative fulfilment through uncoercive labour, are of direct importance in our time.

In relation to dialectical materialism I must confess that many of the intricacies of dialectics were beyond my comprehension. This however did not surprise me as I found myself in good company! Lenin called Bukharin the most brilliant theoretician in the Bolshevik Party but added that "he did not understand dialectics." On the question of materialism, the final judgment comes to rest on the debatable point which came first: mind or matter? A problem I found far beyond my intellectual capacity to resolve. Consequently I would not have termed myself either a materialist or an idealist in that sense, preferring to call myself an agnostic. That did not mean however that I was disinterested in the mind-matter problem, but it did not seem necessary to provide a precise answer to that question in order to adopt an ideological stand. This view combined with progressive disillusionment with the Soviet system brought me closer to the ideas of democratic socialism.

For me any ideology to be relevant in the Indian context had to place at its centre the deprivations of millions of our people and to make the improvement of their lot its primary commitment. In a backward country with capitalism in its early stages, only the State is in a position to undertake the gigantic task of rapid economic development in a planned way. This is an incontestable fact in the light of which, the arguments for socialism become irrefutable. The main challenge was to combine the fastest economic growth with the maximum possible application of socialist values. This is a tremendously complex and difficult process and with circumstances as they were in the country it was difficult to discern which was the best road to take. Among socialists I found much concern to preserve civic and democratic rights as well as the cultural freedom we enjoyed.

But, I asked myself, what happens if one is compelled to make a choice between democracy and rapid economic development? The majority of my friends, I found, maintained a firm allegiance to democratic forms, but I found myself unable to take up so dogmatic a stand, though naturally in an ideal world one would like to see the combination of form and speed. There were two reasons for my differing on this point. I tried to see the problems facing India in their historical perspective. This was extremely depressing since one immediately became aware that even after a life time of dedicated and systematic effort one would eventually die without seeing one's work fulfilled. From this point of view however it was clear that any nation at a particular stage in its development could set itself only a certain number of goals. It is impossible to achieve everything at once. Because of the limitation of human and material resources, priorities have to be decided upon, whether one likes it or not. If any one tries to apply the whole range of democratic socialist ideas in an under-developed country he would be writing himself off from political effectiveness because his aims will not be understood or appreciated by overwhelming majority of people. My own feeling is that one of the major drawbacks of Asian socialist thinking has been that, as a reaction against the communist dictatorial method, too much stress has been laid upon the democratic form closely resembling the western multi-party parliamentary system. In most of the newly developing countries where this has been introduced it could not sustain itself, because the conventions, habits and discipline which are necessary to make the system function effectively were almost non-existent. In India this particular form has persisted so far, not because the Indian people are particularly more suited to it than other nations of Asia and Africa, but simply because the Congress Party which believed in this system, was voted to power with an overwhelming majority in successive general elections and was thus able to provide political stability.

With the alteration of this situation after the fourth general elections has come the real test of the Indian parliamentary system. Only the very bold would predict what the outcome will be. If at any stage of her history the parliamentary system in India is faced with disintegration, what then should be the attitude of the democratic socialists ?

Surrounded by the wreckage of so many parliamentary systems and realizing how easily the sapling of democracy will wilt and die in a harsh and difficult terrain, socialists, in my opinion, cannot afford to put their entire faith in so sophisticated a form but should possess enough imagination to explore other democratic structures, which though perhaps not refined enough for western tastes, would nevertheless instil a feeling of dignity in the individual, providing him with opportunities for democratic discussion and decision at least at lower levels, and inculcating habits of voluntary participation in community life.

It is not only the conduct of governmental affairs in India but personal experiences of working within the democratic socialist party which has caused me to have second thoughts concerning the function of democracy in underdeveloped countries. It seems to me the consciousness of the rights among the people does not generally commensurate with their sense of duty. No major problems can be solved without herculean labour and yet the importance of work and duty gets overlooked in the midst of the din of argument about constitutional rights.

I have gradually and unwillingly been driven to the conclusion, that a regime which might not stick to all subtleties of democratic procedure but which is genuinely serving the interests of the overwhelming majority of the people is more democratic than one with a democratic structure, which is manipulated by the rich and the privileged classes, and which totally fails to unleash in the great mass of people the energies for any constructive or creative endeavour.

While entertaining grave doubts about the efficacy of transplanting western parliamentary systems to India, I have no ambiguity regarding communist dictatorship. I am totally opposed to it. In undeveloped countries communism's main appeal is as a process of rapid industrialization. Stalin achieved this, but he has been condemned for the methods that he had adopted, even by the communists themselves. The indictment of the socialists has been more stringent and I fully share it. The Chinese communists have adopted the same methods. Circumscribed as they are by difficulties both in their national and international spheres, they have failed to solve their basic economic problems and now it is clear that they have no possibility of success unless they radically change their extreme policies. That a communist dictatorship automatically delivers the goods is clearly no longer true and yet it is a known fact that it involves tremendous human suffering and sacrifice, and the trampling underfoot of every value that man has cherished.

A communist dictatorship in India is not likely to be very different from that which faces us across the Himalayan snows. Whatever justification Stalin might have had for his inhuman methods, whether it was the hostility of the capitalist-imperialist countries towards the Soviet Union, or the lack of large-scale foreign assistance, the repetition of such methods cannot by any means be justified in the new historical period in which we live. The removal of poverty is becoming increasingly the concern not only of the individual nations within their territories but of the whole of mankind. A sense of responsibility is spreading among the people of more affluent societies, though admittedly not as quickly as we would wish. Any nation determined to raise itself up and not having an unduly doctrinaire and dogmatic approach and with no intention of involving itself in power politics can certainly hope to soften considerably the sharp edges of economic growth with large-scale foreign assistance. Under these circumstances a communist regime is likely to find itself in greater difficulties than a non-communist one, particularly after the rift between the Soviet Union and Communist China.

I have found James Burnham's plea for combining the struggle for bread and freedom increasingly relevant. For a hungry, illiterate Indian peasant a bowl of rice is of much greater worth than all the freedoms conceived by the intellectuals. Yet those who promise to provide food in exchange for freedom may not be able to fulfil their promise and then those who have relinquished their freedom will no longer have the right even to protest. With the struggle to lift ourselves out of the morass of poverty and degradation, and to ensure for everyone a decent standard of living, has also to be developed a conscious cultivation of more and more freedom, even if it stems from small beginnings.

We often, I think, lose sight of the fact that there is a fundamental difference between western democratic institutions and our own parliamentary democracy. Those in the West are the result of a long and gradual process of organic growth, embracing every aspect of social evolution—economic, scientific, artistic and philosophical. Ours is not an organic growth; we import ideas and techniques and try to meet our pressing needs. With a few exceptions most people are still impelled by traditional habits, thinking and behaviour and this makes the whole process painful and frustrating. The greatest intellectual challenge that we face both individually and socially is the problem of how to preserve what is valuable in our tradition and at the same time to take the fullest advantage of new discoveries in science and technology. It is only upon such a synthesis that the strong foundations of a progressive and forward-looking India can be built and of all the concepts contained in Subhas Chandra Bose's political philosophy this seems to me one of the most enduring.

I discovered then that the ideas of democratic socialism were the most fruitful guide in the resolving of so many demands apparently in conflict with each other—between the individual and society, between national interest and internationalism, between tradition and progress, between democracy and rapid economic development, between "East" and "West".

My response to socialism which came initially as a solution to my personal and emotional needs in relation to the society, soon same to be seen as the means to change society itself. In the international field too, it seemed it was only through socialism that the present crisis in human civilization caused by the continued conflict between the rival power blocs, headed by U.S.A. and U.S.S.R., could be overcome. With the possibility of the survival of the human race overshadowed by threatening mushroom clouds, socialism seemed to nurture within it the seeds of sanity.

To ally oneself with either of the antagonistic forces, capitalism or communism, means becoming a party to a conflict which holds no future for mankind. So far it is true that fatal clash has been avoided and policies of co-existence have been adhered to, partly from the realisation of the horrors which a nuclear war would unleash upon the world, partly owing to the comparative sobriety of the present big power leadership. But a balance of terror and reliance upon the subjective reactions of a handful of men at the top provide a very insecure foundation for World Peace.

It is obvious that entirely new ideas will be required to inspire us to overcome rigidities of ideological dogmatism, to help us to transcend narrow national loyalties and to make certain basic principles the sheet anchor of a new world order, in which the United Nations will inevitably have to play a vital role. One cannot avoid coming to the conclusion that the safety of mankind and the rapid improvement of the economic conditions of two-thirds of world's population cannot effectively be undertaken unless a world government with powerful legislative, judicial, moral and physical authority comes into being. This should be the primary concern of our generation and its achievement is not going to be an easy task. I cannot help asking myself what will be the values on which the new world community will be established. I find the principles of democratic and humanist socialism genuinely applied to international and national problems can show us the only way to extricate ourselves from the present stalemate. It will mean a breakthrough of the thought barriers built up by capitalism and communism, but this no longer seems quite impossible.

Immediately after the second world war the socialist attitude of "double rejection" of capitalism and communism and their proposals for the third alternative was considered to be utopian since all the material powers seemed to be invested in one or other of these two camps. Today however policies of neutralism and non-alignment are eminently respectable and the expanding third force composed of non-aligned nations is being courted by both East and West, since their combined strength has now become a powerful factor in the shaping of international politics. Even in the citadels of capitalism and communism, a realization of the need for change is spreading and some of the fundamental ideas on which the two systems were built are being increasingly subjected to question, especially by the younger generation.

Certainly the transformation will not come easily. It will need a tremendous amount of conviction and sustained, dedicated action of millions throughout the world to prevent a nuclear catastrophe and to usher in a new era. No other ideology has been able to clarify the issues so sharply as socialism and I am convinced that it is the only way to sanity and survival.

Society however is the sum of its individuals, all with their specific problems and needs. In the newly emerging industrial societies like India, with the progressive decline of religious faith, where joint family systems are breaking up and the traditional moral restraints gradually disappearing, the problems of human relationships and of "alienation" are becoming more acute with the passing of time. Contemporary capitalism and communism have not been able to offer any satisfactory solution to this widespread human problem. Dr. Erich Fromm says that "Love is the only sane and satisfactory answer to the problems of human existence," and it is essential that man's social and loving nature should not be separated from his social existence which should become one with it. Neither the "pursuit of private profit" nor "historical necessity" should be the guiding principle of a society, but rather should it be the fostering of that peculiarly human quality—loving; otherwise however materially prosperous a community might be, without love it will, like any deprived individual, disintegrate from within.

Socialism has always made solidarity and comradeship its central motivation. So far, this has meant mainly the struggle against oppression, exploitation and misery in class societies. Where socialists are wielding State power and engaged in the building of a new order, solidarity, human fellowship and love have to be at the centre of socio-economic system. It is only socialists, who by historical tradition have the necessary bent of mind to put man in "his supreme place." For me, although the socialist movement might not always seem to be the manifestation of the highest intelligence, the most sensitive conscience and the greatest honour of our epoch, it has room in its ranks for all those individuals who aspire to make it so. The ideals of democratic socialism satisfy me both emotionally and intellectually; they provide a sense of direction in my life, instilling it with meaning and purpose. Socialism is the true expression of humanism in our time. It does not want to exclude anyone. It gives opportunities to those who want to, and can go ahead, but does not create barriers between them, and those who cannot. It seeks to create one human family, not with fanaticism and avoidable cruelties but with the power of understanding and love and the self-sacrifice of its followers.

PART FOUR

EPILOGUE

"In my end is my beginning." — T. S. Eliot.

By seemingly insignificant events our lives are changed. We turn right instead of left, miss a train, fall ill, talk to a stranger, and after that moment nothing ever is the same again. Often the original reason for the change is forgotten and yet it remains, buried deep under the surface of our conscious lives, a source of renewal for our tarnished ideals, of inspiration for fresh fields of action.

Some experiences in our lives stand out in such brilliance that everything which follows seems colourless and dry. It may not be possible to follow up the experience as we would wish and the whole of our energies may be devoted to some quite different sphere of activity. We may apparently adjust to the new situation, as a lover suffering from unrequited love, will marry the bride of his second choice, while continuing to relive in imagination the precious hours he had spent with his first love. This twilight region between commitment and non-commitment is not for me. It would seem better to live fully in one's second or even third choice of activity than to squander one's energies in dream. At the same time it is equally fruitless to pay lip service to one's commitment and yet not be at all seriously involved.

I once met a woman, a believer in transmigration of souls, who told me that in my previous birth I had lived in Europe. I do not know about that but certainly if I had really wanted to follow my personal interests I would have made it my home. I had no family or other obligations and in Europe there are infinite opportunities for every conceivable pursuit, but I returned to India because I felt my place was there. I had made no promises except to myself and failure to return would not noticeably have affected anyone. Yet for my own satisfaction I could not have remained in Europe. What I could achieve by returning was a secondary matter.

To most people at some time during their lives, there comes, for one reason or another, the conviction that there is no meaning or purpose in existence. We fail in our relationship with others; we seek for love and do not find it, or we lose our job and our sense of security. We become aware of the terrifying limitations of the body. We realise suddenly that we are mortal, that death will be the end of all things.

By good luck I found the love I needed and love brings confidence to face any number of difficulties and disasters. During one period of my life I desperately needed a job but could not find one. Having the urge to work, yet sitting around in enforced idleness, I could appreciate the plight of the unemployed. One feels rejected by the society, flotsam swept to and from in the tide of misfortune. One feels angry and has the irresistible urge to blow up everything around. The frailty of our tenuous hold on life,

"How little while we have to stay
And once departed may return no more."

is brought home forcibly when we are ill. I have known during the violent attack of asthma how my vision of life can be completely, even though temporarily, distorted.

When we have found love and work and are healed of our sickness we no longer have the same feelings as the man who continues to suffer. How far then does our experience of suffering have any lasting relevance in our lives? Certainly we are better able to enter into the sufferings of others for even although we apparently forget painful experiences, everything remains even though at a sub-conscious level and those events which we feel to be of value can be deliberately nourished to add depth and beauty to our lives. In this way I have always valued and cherished my experience in the Bihar village in a symbolic way for it opened up a whole new world which seemed to contain everything I felt to be worthwhile—emotionally, intellectually and spiritually.

Over thirty years afterwards this youthful idealism has perforce been shaped by pragmatism. A single incident impelled me into politics and I am in politics still. Why? I ask myself. Is it for power? For fame? For altruism? Perhaps I am incapable of doing anything else? I still believe that without any effective settlement of the political problems in India no real progress can be achieved, and the problems in this country are of such dimensions that only drastic treatment will have any real effect.

After the romance of the freedom movement and the high

hopes of the pre-independence period, disenchantment swiftly followed, not only with the way independence was brought about but also with the organization of society in free India. Political life since 1947 has been a period of bitter disappointment and frustration and with a depressingly small number of people with the right perspectives and values who would be willing to work as a team.

Nevertheless I have not lost heart. Some equate this with naive idealism on my part. I am convinced that there is enormous potentiality in the Indian people and that in spite of the complexity of her problems, India with right leadership and organization could forge ahead to take her place among the leading nations of the world.

It is the difficulty in finding the leadership in a developing country; the necessity for all who have had the advantage of education and training to use them to the utmost, which has kept me moving in a world for which I am temperamentally unsuited. When I was a boy I wanted to be learned, aloof and reasonably affluent. My natural propensities were leading towards a life in which such desires could have been realised. Now, almost with a vengeance as it were, perhaps to prove my free will and to disprove determinism in human life, I remained unlearned, unaloof and certainly not rich, though in a country of dire poverty I cannot truthfully say I am poor.

In the midst of all the turmoil and anguish of youth, to feather one's own nest when there was so much suffering around seemed completely immoral. In those days I conceived of my life as being short and intense, and consequently, took little positive interest in my personal future either intellectually or economically.

One day I heard a palmist telling a friend of mine "You are very generous. You want to do things for others. For instance, if someone was drowning you would like to jump in and save him. But you cannot swim." Now it seems to me that I could have done well to practise a little swimming before I leapt in at the deep end. As it is the most important decisions I have taken I have arisen from a persistent negativism. Sheer lack of choice led me to take up journalism. For unquenchable curiosity I read in any case, and with a little systematic reading I thought, I could possibly write as well. At least anything I could do would be made available for others. That was my ideal from the beginning, and remains so.

A man cannot enter politics without some consideration of the meaning of power and its effect on the individual. That power corrupts is a truism. Power and fame raise the man in the sight of others and willy nilly in his own. This can easily lead to inflated ideas of his own importance. Only if he is able to relate to aims and ideals beyond himself can he keep his head. It is really a question of how much he can digest. If the head and the heart are working together the ability to preserve a balanced view will be so much the greater. When a politician has lost his vision he may as well retire.

While the political field is the main area for a change in the developing country, severe limitations are imposed on politicians in a democracy, since in a tradition-bound society any unorthodox behaviour on the part of a public worker could work to his disadvantage. Some of my friends have suggested that if I wish to continue my public work I should omit the chapter on love in this book. They may be right to be apprehensive. It is true that you cannot change people's lives if you alienate them, but I see politics as a transforming force not only in the economic and political sphere, but as affecting the whole of life. I may be a political worker, but I am also an individual seeking answers to the problems of existence. Those answers cannot be found without experiments; the experiments in themselves may contain nothing which is true for me but they are nevertheless a necessary part of the search. It seems to me although isolated incidents may appear to be socially unorthodox, it is the underlying direction which we take which is important.

My attitude in this has to a large extent been influenced by Gandhi, who did not want politics and religion to be separated. In our secular State substitute "philosophy of life" for religion and the theory holds good as far as I am concerned. I also think that what might be concerned "wicked" or "immoral" by the older generation (of which I am almost a qualifying member) is less likely to be regarded as such by today's young people. Many of the conflicts will be theirs and they may be able to identify themselves with situation which troubled me when I was their age. If this happens then it will be more worthwhile than any temporary advantage I may have derived as a politician by suppressing facts.

I want India to be a land of synthesis in which all the contradictory elements are reconciled in our political, economic and cultural life. At this stage of human evolution this will be the greatest challenge, not only in India but all over the world. All countries faced with conflict between religious communities, between black and white, between rich and poor, between the old ways and the new have to work for their reconciliation or face disaster. If India could achieve such a synthesis she will have something to give to the world. With her tradition, her enormous potential in human and material resources she could do it—but certainly not if she continues as she has done in the last twenty years.

Only through a radical transformation in outlook and by massive social action by the whole of our people can we begin to embark on the work to be done. After the 1971 Indo-Pakistan conflict and the emergence of independent Bangladesh, it seems that the country has turned a corner and a new confidence has been generated. We are living in highly exciting and stimulating times. We are in control of our own destiny, architects of our own future. I would like to play some small part in helping to bring a new India to birth. In that would be my fulfilment.

INDEX